Diary of a Mall Santa

৪০০৪

The Truth,
the HO! HO! HO! Truth,
and Nothing but the Truth.

By Stewart Scott

Diary of a Mall Santa

Copyright © 2014 Stewart Scott

All Rights Reserved. Published 2014.

No part of this publication may be reproduced, distributed, or transmitted in any form or by any means, including photocopying, recording, or other electronic or mechanical methods, without the prior written permission of the publisher, except in the case of brief quotations embodied in critical reviews and certain other noncommercial uses permitted by copyright law. For permission requests, write to the publisher, addressed "Attention: Permissions Coordinator," at the address below.

First published by Faith Books & MORE

ISBN 978-1-939761-29-3

Printed in the United States of America on acid-free paper.

Faith Books & MORE
3255 Lawrenceville-Suwanee Rd.
Suite P250
Suwanee, GA 30024
publishing@faithbooksandmore.com
faithbooksandmore.com

Ordering Information:
Quantity sales. Special discounts are available on quantity purchases by corporations, associations, and others. For details, contact the publisher at the address above.

Orders by U.S. trade bookstores and wholesalers. Please contact Ingram Book Company: Tel: (800) 937-8000.
Email: orders@ingrambook.com or visit ipage.ingrambook.com.

The author is not liable or responsible, to any person, or entity, for any and all claims, demands, damages, causes of action, suits in equity of whatever kind or nature, caused or alleged to have been caused, directly or indirectly, by the information contained in this book or the author's past or future negligence or wrongful acts.

*T*he stories in this diary are true.
The names have been changed
to avoid embarrassing my guests.
Some of the stories have been
discreetly embellished, and seasoned
with pinches of humor, compassion,
and traces of cynicism.

DEDICATION

This book is dedicated to Jean, my wife, and our five
children. They are the joy of my life.
More than forty years of raising children has
equipped me for being Santa.

ACKNOWLEDGMENTS

Thank you for believing, Mrs. Krueger.

ಸಂಬಂ

I also want to thank my good friends,
Rob McManamy, Susan Heitsch, Sally Maloni,
Charlie Hasser, and Nancy Hall –
all of whom carefully read my manuscript,
caught errors, and suggested creative flourishes
that made the stories more appealing.
And thank you to the parents, grandparents,
aunts and uncles who entrusted
thousands of children to my care.

APOLOGIA

During my time as Santa, I met with more than 2,500 children and adults over 34 days. By the end of the day on Christmas Eve, I had recorded 122 noteworthy stories. These stories were out of the ordinary and worth including in my diary.

Some of the stories exposed less than perfect parenting skills. While they were important to include, I came to realize that my wife and I had made almost all of these mistakes with our children – and they were not ruined for life.

I apologize to parents who feel I am poking fun at their human foibles when they bring their children to Santa for a grand audience.

FOREWORD

SANTA GETS HIS SUIT

"Look, Daddy," Zuzu exclaimed, "teacher says, 'Every time a bell rings an angel gets his wings.' "

"That's right, that's right," George responds, as he winks and smiles at an invisible Clarence.
(Dialog from: *It's a Wonderful Life.*)

Several months before Christmas, the *phone rang* one afternoon and it wasn't long before I got my Santa suit and the job of a lifetime.

The call was from the general manager of a regional shopping mall outside of Chicago. "Do you know anyone who would like to play Santa Claus this year?" she asked, sounding a little desperate.

I didn't have to think long before I told her I would love the job.

The scenario reminded me of a family Christmas Eve more than 30 years ago when our children were very young. The doorbell rang about 8 p.m.; we were not expecting guests. When I opened the door Santa and Mrs. Santa were waiting, illuminated only by the dim porch light. They came bearing gifts for Alison, Jon and Gale; and they knew each of our children by name. Santa and his wife seemed so real that I glanced in the front yard, halfway expecting to see a sleigh and eight tiny reindeer. To this day I have no idea who those people were. Ever since that experience, I've wanted to return the favor and play Santa Claus for countless children.

I had plenty of questions. Would I get any training? What should I do if a child asks for scores of expensive gifts? What about teenagers? Will they give me any trouble? Do I have to join a Santa Claus union? In time my questions were answered, yet no amount of coaching could adequately prepare me for this job. I had to learn and react with each new day.

Weeks later, when I met my first group of visitors to Santa Land, I learned that Santa becomes a real life ***angel*** for the boys, girls and other believers who visit, sit on my lap and share their Christmas wishes.

INTRODUCTION

*T*he stories you will read in this diary are based on my actual experiences. Some of the stories are heartwarming; some are heartbreaking; some are a bit cynical and irreverent; and some are funny. But all are true.

There is a story about nine-year-old Isabel, a little girl who asked only for a home for her parents. Nothing for herself. You will read about a group of children who brought along a *Toys "R" Us* catalog, and most of the items were circled. When I suggested that the cost of the gifts might be too expensive, one little boy said, "That's okay. You're Santa. You'll bring them." And there was the middle-aged woman, short and round, with a mischievous smile; she insisted on sitting on my lap for her picture with Santa. After the photo was taken, she whispered in my ear, "You have 200 pounds of FUN sitting on your lap."

Being Santa Claus for a major mall was a new experience for me. I had no idea what to expect, even though I had researched the assignment.

I believe the most valuable legacy a parent can leave behind is happy, well-adjusted children. Those children will go on to emulate their parents.

Children need positive encouragement, and that is one of Santa's jobs. They need to be told they are loved and that they are good. When we constantly tell children they are bad, they will be bad. It's a self-fulfilling prophecy.

Many people think that Santa personifies the rampant secular commercialism we have come to dislike about the Christmas season. It depends on Santa. Saint Nicholas, the original Santa, was born in the third century. His parents died from an epidemic at an early age, and Nicholas inherited their great wealth. Because he was a devout Christian, he followed the biblical admonition to, "Sell everything you have and give your money to the poor." He had a heart for children, sailors at sea, and other people in need. He made a huge difference in the lives of hundreds of people and his example should inspire us to do the same today.

Stewart Scott

Stewart Scott

34 days before Christmas

FIRST VISITORS, *10:45 a.m.*

*T*his was my first day on the job and I wasn't sure what to expect.

Santa Land was decked out in colorful holiday splendor. More than 1,000 square feet, located in the heart of the mall, were decorated with Santa's workshops. There were mechanical elves, ice skating penguins on artificial ponds, fully decorated Christmas trees, imitation snow, gingerbread men, and a winding path from the entrance to Santa's grand throne. A white picket fence surrounded my kingdom, and I was the crown prince of the party. Everybody treated me like royalty.

When children weren't waiting in line to see me, I was on my feet waving to people and noisily shaking my jingle bells. Often, I ventured out from my sanctuary and personally greeted people. Practically

Diary of a Mall Santa

everyone waved back and called out my name. After all, Santa is a beloved age-old icon.

Today the mall was a shopping destination for a busload of mentally disabled adults. I noticed a man in his twenties pushing an older friend in a wheelchair through the entrance to Santa Land. They were alone. No children were in sight when I invited them to join me. The man in the wheelchair had a drooping Fu Manchu mustache and wavy, shoulder-length brown hair. While both men appeared to be perfectly normal, it wasn't until we engaged in conversation that I learned they were mentally challenged. I was flattered when the younger man said they were there for a picture with me.

I told both men how happy I was to see them, and how pleased I was that they were visiting the mall. A normal, give-and-take conversation was out of the question. As we posed in front of the Christmas tree for a picture, the man in the wheelchair gripped me tightly around the waist. While he was easily in his 40s, I saw the innocent eyes of a child who was thrilled beyond belief to be with Santa. When I spoke to him and asked him questions, tears welled up in his eyes. He was too overcome with the joy of the moment to say a single word.

From that point on I knew that I had taken on a job with monumental responsibilities.

ಸಂಧ

TALL TALE, *11:18 a.m.*

The quality and quantity of Christmas gifts is often a barometer of the economy. When times are tough, parents often limit their children to one or two presents.

One family must have hit the jackpot, because Gina presented me with a very long list rolled up like a scroll. Later in the day, I measured the taped-together pieces of paper. At 5-1/2 feet, the list was longer than the girl was tall. It included 141 gift ideas, and many of them were expensive. In fact, just to help me out, Gina included the retail prices of many of the items.

Gina and her mother did not appear to be particularly wealthy. No fur coats and Mom wasn't decked out in diamonds. When she handed me the scroll, I watched for a reaction from Mom. I think she was a willing participant in the Santa shakedown scheme.

If the little girl is disappointed on Christmas morning, I hope she doesn't blame it on Santa. The bundle of 141 gifts wouldn't even fit down the chimney.

෨෧

SOILED BRITCHES, *1:05 p.m.*

Not all stories were heartwarming.

A four-year-old boy approached me, but stopped short of my chair.

I held out both hands and asked if he would like to sit on my lap.

With a dejected frown, he said, "I pooped in my pants."

"Well," I said, "maybe we should just talk from where you are." After all, I thought, this Santa suit needs to stay fresh and clean for the next month.

"They're gonna beat me," he said.

The words "beat" and "child" don't seem to go together. Besides, I don't think "beating" will solve the problem of pooping in your pants. I doubt if he did it just to upset his parents. I always thought that carrying around the smelly load was punishment enough.

ಜೋಡ

A BETTER SOLUTION, *2:27 p.m.*

"Santa, tell Johnny he's a BAD boy. If he doesn't straighten up, you're not going to bring him anything for Christmas." The boy's mother shouted instructions as she presented her embarrassed five-year-old child.

The youngster stood before me, head bowed in shame, awaiting his sentence.

I listened to the mother, but did not respond to her instructions.

I lifted Johnny onto my lap and began a quiet conversation. I asked him how old he was and what grade he was in. Johnny answered my questions and we began a short conversation about Christmas and what he wanted this year.

Diary of a Mall Santa

"Johnny," I said, looking him straight in the eye and holding him by both shoulders, "you're a good boy and Santa's very proud of you."

Johnny looked startled. I don't think anyone had ever told him he was good before.

The encounter reminded me of a quote I heard years ago: "Treat people (and children) as if they were what they ought to be and you help them become what they are capable of being." The author was Johann Wolfgang von Goethe.

ಬಂಡ

Stewart Scott

33 days before Christmas

TEENAGERS, *4:15 p.m.*

Among many young teenage girls, there is a small corner of their hearts that still believes in Santa.

Today three teenage girls shyly ventured into the inner sanctum of Santa Land. One of the bolder ones asked, "Can we get our picture taken with Santa?"

"Sure," I replied. "Would you like to gather around my chair or would you like the picture taken standing in front of the Christmas tree?"

They chose to gather around my chair.

You should know that a mechanical elf works his mischief between my oversized Santa chair and the nearby Christmas tree. All day long he swivels to and fro as if he's placing ornaments on the tree. Some of the children think he's one of the original elves, and they stare at him in disbelief. The teenagers didn't pay attention to the elf. Perhaps they thought he was harmless.

Diary of a Mall Santa

The four of us were gathered in and around my chair in a cozy pose with arms around each other when the pesky elf made an abrupt clockwise turn. His hand nudged the rear end of one of the teenagers.

She jumped. "OHMYGOD!" she said, not realizing the elf was behind her.

They left laughing and smiling, yet a little embarrassed by the awkward moment.

ಸಃಡ

CRITICS, *5:07 p.m.*

"Hey Santa! You're anorexic," a voice shouted from the nearby escalator.

I looked to my right and saw a middle-aged woman with arms the size of Virginia hams. Several of her friends laughed as she heckled Santa.

Some people expect me to match the vivid description of Santa Claus in Clement Moore's famous poem, *'Twas the Night Before Christmas.* One stanza of the poem reads:

He was chubby and plump,
   A right jolly old elf,

And I laughed when I saw him,
in spite of myself.

Sorry folks, I'm not going on an eating binge just to gain weight for the Christmas season.

ಬಂಡ

ELECTRA SET ME STRAIGHT, *5:31 p.m.*

A stout little girl, about four years old, inched toward me. She didn't smile. In fact, she had a defiant look on her young face.

Her name was Electra, although she bore no resemblance to a young Carmen Electra. She looked tough and much too street smart for a little girl.

"And what do you want Santa to bring you for Christmas?" I asked cheerfully, trying to introduce a pleasant mood.

"A DOWLG," she growled.

When pets are requested I usually say, "Dogs and cats don't like to travel in my sleigh. Sometimes they get sick and throw up on the presents."

I thought the comment might make her smile.

Before I could complete the sentence, she said, "I didn't say DOG, I SAID DOLL!"

"A doll! That's a wonderful idea. Much better than a dog."

ೋఌ

DON'T PRESS YOUR LUCK, *6:18 p.m.*

Nina settled comfortably on my lap. When she leaned her head on my shoulder and sighed, she gave the impression that she was not about to leave any time soon. She made me feel as if she had been looking forward to this moment of warmth and security for months. I learned that Nina was nine years old, loved school, her friends and her teacher, and will be satisfied with almost any gift for Christmas. She was more interested in spending time with Santa than listing off dozens of gift ideas.

The time flew by because our conversation was spontaneous.

Finally, I asked Nina if she liked cookies.

"Oh yes," she said, "and my favorite is chocolate."

"Mine too!" I said. "Say, Nina, could you do me a little favor?" Her eyes brightened. "Will you ask your mom to bake chocolate cookies and maybe you could leave me one on Christmas Eve, along with a glass of milk."

"My mom's a terrible cook," she said, "but I'll leave you a glass of milk."

"Milk will be just fine, and how about a carrot for my reindeer?"

"Don't press your luck, Santa," she said, with a twinkle in her eye.

ಬಾಡಿ

SANTA'S GAFFE, *6:43 p.m.*

Just when I thought I was feeling comfortable in my Santa role, I put my foot in my mouth. I have had many years of parenting experience, but our youngest child is 25 and it's been a long time since I've shopped for little girls and boys.

Here was my blunder: a cute little girl with curly blonde hair and bright blue eyes was warmly dressed for the winter weather. Her stocking cap was embroidered with the name "Dora," and I assumed it was her name.

"I'll bet I know what your name is," I said to the child – "Dora!"

The mother reminded me that "Dora" is a brand name.

I felt like a real idiot later that evening when I told my wife what I had done. Jean was very aware of the Dora brand. She shops for our granddaughters.

Just call me Santa Dork.

ೲಬ

32 days before Christmas

SANTA MEETS ISABEL, *2:20 p.m.*

Most of the young visitors I saw on the days approaching Christmas were similar. I asked them to sit on my lap and then I introduced several questions to establish a closer relationship. After we got to know one another, I asked them what they wanted

Stewart Scott

Santa to deliver on Christmas Eve. Every now and then an extraordinary child melted my heart.

Today I met Isabel. She was a reserved little girl, tall for her age. She had an oval face, dark hair and eyes, and a light-olive complexion. Isabel also had a soft, engaging smile that made me feel like I had known her for years.

Isabel was Hispanic, but I detected no trace of a Spanish accent. I asked her how old she was and what grade she was in before I asked her about Christmas gifts. All she asked for was a home for her parents and a job for her unemployed daddy. She asked for nothing for herself.

Most children demanded my attention with long lists of expensive gift ideas, but not Isabel.

I was struck by her selfless maturity. I tried to respond to her Christmas wishes as tears began to well up in my eyes.

"Isabel," I said, "I can tell there is a lot of love in your family, and that is one of the most precious gifts of all."

Diary of a Mall Santa

"May I have a hug?" I asked.
She responded quickly. I knew she would.

ಸಂಬ

YOU CAN ASSUME THAT, *4:08 p.m.*

A teenage couple slowly walked through Santa Land hand-in-hand, and we learned that they wanted their picture taken with Santa.

The girl sat on the right-hand armrest and her boyfriend sat opposite her on the other side of the chair. I was in the middle. Neither of them could have been more than 18 or 19 years old.

They were very specific with their Christmas wish. They wanted a puppy and they intended to name him Kevin.

"Before I agree with your request, may I assume you've been good?" I asked, looking back and forth at both the teenage girl and her boyfriend.

"You can assume that," she said, as she slowly stood up and displayed her swollen pregnant belly.

I guess "good" is a relative term.

ಸಂಬ

Stewart Scott

THE INVISIBLE MAN, *7:35 p.m.*

When my Santa shift ended at 7 p.m., I headed for my dressing room in a vacant store in a remote corner of the mall. The room had all the amenities I needed: a bathroom, a place to hang my clothes, a table for lunch, and peace and quiet. It took about a half-hour to change from my complicated Santa suit into street clothes. I also had to scrub the rouge and snow-white eyebrow paint from my face. I felt skinny again when I finally removed the pillow from under my T-shirt.

In a relatively short period of time, I transformed myself from the immensely popular Santa Claus to just plain Stew.

I could have left the mall via the hidden passageways that customers didn't know about, but I chose to walk through the mall and observed the children who were clamoring to see me earlier in the day.

As the sound of each footstep reverberated off the marble floors, I felt like an invisible man. I felt like Bilbo Baggins in the *The Hobbit* once he slipped the magic ring onto his finger, only I didn't feel empowered — just invisible. The adoring children no longer took notice. I was no longer Santa, the source of their joy. I was just another guy walking through the mall.

I smiled softly when I saw the children who sat on my lap earlier in the day, but they no longer smiled back. The feeling was surreal, but it allowed me to come down from the high of being Santa.

I can't wait until tomorrow.

31 days before Christmas

A GREAT SADNESS, *3:47 p.m.*

Eleven-year-old Tanya came in to see me. Her aunt and grandmother waited in the background. She had long blonde hair, pale blue eyes, and a pensive expression on her face.

Stewart Scott

"What are you thinking about for Christmas this year?" I asked, after we got acquainted. I expected a list of gift ideas.

Instead she said, "I would like my mom's jaw to feel better. This will be her last Christmas."

Wow, I thought. What a heavy burden for a child to bear. "Is there anything you would like to talk to Santa about?" I asked, not knowing how I could begin to assuage her sadness.

"No," she said, as she shook her head.

I held her hands in my left hand and my right hand rested softly against her shoulder. We snuggled a little closer. People identify Santa with his boisterous Ho! Ho! Hos! and his jolly demeanor. Tanya simply wanted someone to hear her story and share her sorrow. She needed someone to allow her to be sad in a season that is otherwise filled with joy.

"How can I help?" I asked.

She shrugged her shoulders. No words were exchanged, yet we understood each other's feelings.

I hear thousands of stories from children and adults; only a few are recorded in this diary. The encounter with Tanya will stay with me for a long time.

ಬಂಡ

DOG-LESS DOGHOUSE, *4:41 p.m.*

Maria was an energetic six-year-old, eager for the coming of Christmas. Her face was round with a broad smile and slight gaps between her teeth.

When I asked what was on her Christmas list, she told me only one thing. She wanted a doghouse. I was relieved. Had she asked for a dog, I would have had to steer her away from that idea. Santa isn't supposed to come close to promising live pets.

"A doghouse," I said, "that's an interesting idea. Is your dog big or little?"

"He's a little dog," she said, "and his name is Hoagie."

"Is he rambunctious?" I asked. "Does he like to run around the house?"

"Oh, yes! He does," she quickly said, as if she knew everything about little Hoagie.

"Well then, I think a doghouse is a fine idea. It will keep Hoagie from running around the house all day long."

We shared a few other gift ideas before she leaped off my lap with her new coloring book in hand. Other children were not waiting in line, so I thought I should tell Maria's mother about the doghouse request.

"Where does she get that idea?" the mother said, not looking surprised. "We don't even have a dog."

Either Maria just has a vivid imagination or she is a budding fiction writer.

ಐಚ್ಯ

WHOSE BIRTHDAY IS IT ANYWAY? *5:20 p.m.*

Some people have lost touch with the true meaning of Christmas.

Today a forty-something woman brought her three young children in for a visit with Santa. After the pictures were taken, she ushered her clan toward the exit door. Before leaving, she turned to face me again and shouted loud enough for everyone to hear, "HAVE A HAPPY BIRTHDAY, SANTA."

ഇരു

30 days before Christmas

ADULT VISITOR, *11:07 a.m.*

When traffic was slow, I often ventured into the mall. I didn't just wave to children. Everyone, regardless of age, received my Christmas greeting.

Today a woman entered my Santa domain by the exit door. She was short, curvy and looked to be about 50 years old. She had a bright smile that lighted up the room and a mischievous gleam in her eyes. Her age didn't stop her from requesting an audience with Santa. That's okay. If she wanted to suspend reality, I was willing to be the Santa Claus of her childhood dreams.

Margaret was there for a picture with Santa. I asked if she would like her picture taken in front of the Christmas tree or sitting on the arm of my Santa chair.

"I'd like to sit on your LAP," she insisted, "but I'd probably break your legs."

"Santa has strong legs, Hop right up."

We smiled for the camera with our arms around each other while the photographer worked his magic.

Then Margaret hugged me and whispered in my ear, "You've got 200 pounds of FUN sitting on your lap."

ೞಣ

SANTA STINKS, *1:55 p.m.*

"Santa, you stink," a precocious little boy said with authority.

"That's because the last child had a surprise in his pants," I said. "He sat right here," patting my right knee.

The new boy decided to relay his Christmas wishes from a short distance away.

There are hazards to being a mall Santa.

ೞಣ

Diary of a Mall Santa

ROCK STAR, *2:31 p.m.*

Three young children and their father were gathered not far from my dressing room as I made my way to Santa Land this afternoon, after a short break. When I spotted the kids, I rang my jingle bells vigorously to capture their attention. They ran full speed toward me, and I dropped down on both knees to receive their generous hugs. The father looked on approvingly. After talking to the children and telling them how happy I was to see them, I rose slowly to shake hands with their father.

"I feel like a rock star," I said.

"You ARE a rock star," he replied.

"I take this job seriously," I told the father.

When children demonstrated such amazing love for a jolly fat man in a bright red suit with an oversized, scratchy beard, you had better not take your responsibilities lightly. When innocent children put their complete trust in a total stranger, you had better not violate their faith.

ಐಡ

Stewart Scott

SPOILED VISITOR, *5:12 p.m.*

A well-dressed four-year-old boy climbed up on my lap, looking very confident. His black hair was neatly combed, and he wore a white Oxford cloth shirt with a buttoned-down collar. He knew exactly what he wanted for Christmas.

He rattled off gift demands preceded by a series of, "I WANNA, I WANNA, I WANNAS."

At the close of our conversation, I made my usual comments. "I'll bet you're a good boy," I said. "I know you help around the house, pick up your toys, and put your clothes away." After all, Santa is supposed to know everything.

"I'm only a kid. Of course I don't do those things," he said without hesitating.

"How old do you think you need to be before you start helping out?" I replied, just as quickly.

"When I'm an ADULT." His tone was defiant. I wasn't going to win this debate.

"Let me see if I understand," I said. "You want me to bring you dozens of presents for Christmas, but you don't want to help out at home – not even pickup your own toys after you've played with them."

The boy folded his arms tightly across his chest and scowled, "I'll think about it."

℘

29 days before Christmas

TERRIFIED CHILD, *3:10 p.m.*

The child was petrified. I've seen the look many times. She was three years old and clearly did not want to be anywhere near a man in a Santa costume. I understood; the grandmother did not.

The grandmother pushed the child toward me several times, saying, "Go see Santa. You said you wanted to see him, now GO!"

The child screamed in fear. I held out my hand and showed her the mall coloring book, but nothing I could do or say would allay her fear. In frustration the grandmother said, "I give up. You're just mean!" She directed her harsh comments to the distraught child.

Trying to be a peacemaker, I said to the grandmother, "It's common for a three-year-old to be terrified of Santa. She's just afraid."

The grandmother shot back, "She's not afraid. She's an evil witch."

Santa has to stay in character, so I could not say what I felt like saying.

Sarah Chana Dadcliffe, M. Ed., C. Psych. Assoc. said it best. "Whatever you say goes deep into their little subconscious minds. Deep, deep down, where it will haunt them for the rest of their lives."

ಸಂಬ

CELL PHONE HOME, *4:16 p.m.*

I witnessed the revelation of a new invention today. It happened before my very eyes. It might revolutionize the cell phone industry, but I haven't figured out how to patent the idea.

A mother in her mid-30s, attractive and buxom, clicked off picture after picture of her four-year-old

Diary of a Mall Santa

son with her fancy cell phone camera. She worked with the efficiency of Brenda Starr on a photo assignment. When she was satisfied with her photos, the cell phone disappeared in the blink of an eye. On closer examination, I discovered she had tucked the camera away – safely and securely inside her bra.

My concentration is usually 100% focused on the children, but the woman's slight-of-hand maneuver diverted my attention. At first I thought she was a magician.

She wore a dark orange, low-cut tank top, and a rectangular shape was clearly visible inside her bra, like an oversized pacemaker. I didn't get a chance to watch her retrieve the phone to answer a call – a maneuver that no doubt would have required special dexterity.

I wondered if she ever sets the ringtone to vibrate? I wondered how many women would see the brilliance of this idea and start using their bras as holsters for cell phones? It would be a lot more convenient than tossing a phone into a crowded purse.

೧೧೦೩

Stewart Scott

FAVORITE CHRISTMAS SONGS, *5:47 p.m.*

Susan was an enthusiastic seven-year-old with a beaming smile. After telling me what she wanted for Christmas, she launched into a list of questions. "Does Rudolph really have a red nose? What does he like to eat? Where do the reindeer stay during the day?"

Then, she started telling me her favorite Christmas songs, starting with *Rudolph the Red-Nosed Reindeer* followed by *Jingle Bells* and others. She entertained me with lines from several tunes.

At a brief pause in her non-stop monolog, I asked, "Do you know what my favorite Christmas song is? *Joy to the World.*"

"Never heard of it," she said.

ಸಿಡ

Diary of a Mall Santa

28 days before Christmas

MY DADDY IS NAUGHTY, *1:45 p.m.*

A soft-spoken little girl sat on my lap today; she was about seven years old and tall for her age. She didn't smile or look adoringly at Santa. Her dark hair was pulled back in a ponytail and she bore a sullen, distant expression. I think she just wanted someone to hold her.

I asked her the normal questions, such as, "How old are you?" and, "What are you thinking about for Christmas this year?"

She didn't have an exhaustive list of gift ideas. She asked for dolls and toys, like most seven-year-old girls.

Near the end of our conversation, I looked into her eyes and said, "I can tell just by looking into your eyes that you are a very good little girl."

She said sorrowfully, "But my daddy is naughty."

"What happened?" I asked. "What did your daddy do?"

She mumbled quietly. I couldn't understand her words. I didn't want to say – could you speak a little louder? Santa can't hear you.

So instead I asked, "How does that make you feel?"

"It hurts," she said.

I couldn't imagine that a seven-year-old girl could relate to psychological pain, yet I'm sure she had experienced it. What if she was trying to tell me about sexual abuse? What could I do? I wasn't even sure what she was saying.

Santa is the guy who makes dreams come true, yet there was nothing I could do for that sweet, defenseless child.

After a warm hug from Santa, she returned to her mother, and the next child ran quickly to sit on my lap.

This was only my sixth day on the job, and I had no idea how to intervene on the child's behalf – but I started asking for advice later that day. In the future,

I will encourage the child to talk to a teacher. They are required by law to report suspected abuse.

ಸಾಡ

KISS FOR SANTA, *3:19 p.m.*

Today part of my family visited me at the mall. We planned a cozy group picture with Jean on my lap, Tina and baby Joey sitting next to me, and my son Mark and his mother-in-law, Agnes, standing and flanking the chair.

We were a festive group, filled with the Christmas spirit. This was going to be fun for everyone. Smiles abounded.

The elf photographer was a college sophomore, very organized and efficient.

As she stood before us with her camera, my wife planted a big kiss right on my mouth.

The photographer did not know she was my wife. She thought she was some stranger in the mall, who decided to make her move on Santa.

The elf was tempted to call Security and have my wife reprimanded.

When she learned that Jean was my wife, not a total stranger, we all enjoyed a hearty laugh.

ಸಃಚ

BAIT AND SWITCH, *4:58 p.m.*

Madelyn was bubbling over with excitement as she ran up to see me. She was six years old with short dark hair and a radiant smile that lighted up the Santa set. I didn't have to ask her what she wanted for Christmas. She burst forth with her ideas. "I want a pony," she said.

"You mean a real pony?" I asked. "The kind that goes 'Wheeee!'" I did my best to imitate the whinnying sound of a horse or pony.

"Yes!" she exclaimed, "a real pony."

"You know, Madelyn," I said, "Ponies don't like to travel in my sleigh. They're afraid of heights. Maybe you should talk to Mom or Dad first."

"Then how about a hamster?" she said, without skipping a beat.

Diary of a Mall Santa

I think little Madelyn should be in sales some day. She is savvy to the bait and switch technique.

ఎనికా

27 days before Christmas

THE TRIO, *2:42 p.m.*

*M*ost of the children were delightful, but every now and then the tables turned. Such was the case with the horde I call "The Trio."

At first glance the family looked like many others: an anxious mother, three reasonably well-dressed children and a father who chose to stay in the background and take pictures of his brood in action.

My first sign of a problem was when the oldest child, a boy about seven years old, approached me with a *Toys "R" Us* catalog. Before I could ask my typical Santa questions, he started leafing through the catalog like a speed-reader on steroids, pointing out dozens of circled items. "Santa, I want this" and

"Santa I want that," he said, as he raced through every page of the catalog.

I obliged him by saying – "Yes, those are good ideas." I didn't know what danger awaited.

When he was through, he passed the catalog on to one of his sisters, like two runners in a high-stakes relay. She continued by pointing out each item she wanted in the same tattered catalog. Again, I tried to play the good Santa and listened with interest. As she circled new items, sometimes costing hundreds of dollars, her mother looked on and laughed approvingly.

When the third child made her way to my lap, she picked up where her sister left off. I did a quick calculation; these kids wanted thousands of dollars worth of expensive toys and there was no end in sight.

When this child was satisfied that I understood her demands, the boy returned. In the brief interim, he had thought of other gift ideas and this might be his only chance to share his insatiable needs with Santa.

Diary of a Mall Santa

Then the catalog was passed on to one of the girls for a second run at Santa. Would this ever end? In the meantime, about 15 other children were waiting in line, observing the trio working Santa for everything they could. The mother thought the tag team was hilarious. She couldn't see the scowl beneath my beard.

Then the boy returned a third time, catalog in hand, ready to add more gifts to his list. "You're asking for some expensive items," I told the boy.

"That's okay," he said. "You're Santa. You'll bring them."

"Don't get your hopes up," I answered, as I nudged him off my lap with one hand and motioned to another waiting child to come forward.

The gifts he was asking for were expensive, but his expression was priceless.

ഭാരു

SECRET AGENT, *3:21 p.m.*

It was not unusual to see 10 year olds in Santa Land, yet Jason seemed a little out of place. Maybe because he seemed older than 10. Jason was an athletic-looking African American, well dressed with angular features, and he wore glasses with bold, black frames.

"Santa," he said, as he handed me a neatly folded piece of paper, "this list is for your eyes only." His tone was serious, like a secret agent, and he spoke with the authority of someone much older.

The list included a football, several NFL jerseys and six other items – all carefully printed.

I glanced at his list, and then looked up toward his mother. I wondered if she was aware of the secret list. She looked on impassively. I think Jason was testing the system. He was going to find out once and for all if Santa was the real deal.

Now I know how Kris Kringle felt in *Miracle on 34th Street.* Susan (played by Natalie Wood in the original movie version) asked for a three-bedroom home in suburbia with a swing set in the backyard. In the end, Kris Kringle (the real Santa Claus) came through, and everyone lived happily ever after.

Diary of a Mall Santa

In my world, Santa's powers only go so far – then I have to turn to my higher power, in the hopes that all will turn out well for my young friend.

ℬℭ

SPEAKING IN TONGUES, *4:33 p.m.*

The child looked like any other 10-year-old when she and her mother approached me. I fully expected a rewarding give-and-take conversation with the young lady, until she sat on my lap and started speaking in a strange, incomprehensible language. She babbled on and on in what seemed to be a foreign tongue, as if I could understand every word of her monologue.

"Morga schmorga brakin cratchet," she said, "kupa largo meda makin, bla, bla, bla."

She made absolutely no sense, yet she spoke with articulate authority.

"What's your name?" she asked, as she shifted abruptly from incoherent babbling to perfect English.

"My name is Santa, Santa Claus," I answered.

"Why you lie?" she said accusingly, "WHY YOU LIE?"

"B-b-b-but," I stammered, "everybody calls me Santa," my standard retort.

"WHY YOU LIE?" she shouted, attracting the attention of the other children waiting in line.

I didn't know where this conversation was headed, but I wanted out fast.

As I look back, I'm sure the little girl had some sort of mental impairment, but she might have been more in touch with reality than most of the other children.

If she comes back again next year, I'm just going to tell her my name is Stewart.

ଛଠଃ

26 days before Christmas

YOUR SECRET IS SAFE, *3:37 p.m.*

Isabel returned today. She was the beautiful nine-year-old Hispanic girl who asked only for a house for her parents when she visited me the first time. The family lived in the basement of a small house in a poor section of town.

As I helped her up on my lap, she smiled and asked if I remembered her name.

"How can I forget you Isabel?" I said. "You made quite an impression on me."

We chatted for a while, like old friends. Isabel and I bonded like a loving grandfather and his charming granddaughter, yet we hardly knew each other.

"Are you the real Santa?" Isabel asked with a coy smile.

"Everyone calls me Santa," I replied for the second time today -- hoping my answer would put the question to rest.

She engulfed me with a warm hug and whispered, "Your secret is safe with me."

ಸಂಆ

STONE FACE, *4:30 p.m.*

Jason's mother looked like her face had been chiseled out of a block of granite into a permanent frown. The sides of her mouth turned down naturally. If her mug had been sculpted on Mount Rushmore, her expression would have cast an everlasting pallor on the throngs of visitors. Even if she tried to smile, she would still look angry.

Jason sat on my lap for a visit and a picture, but his mom was not happy with his dour expression. She demanded a smile, and Jason didn't comply.

"Why do you look so mad?" his mother demanded.

I took one look at the mother and then looked at Jason, and discovered that his frown was an enduring part of his DNA, inherited from his stone-faced mother.

Some things you just have to accept.

ఎఁ

TICKET TO RIDE, *5:47 p.m.*

When Charles ambled confidently into Santa Land, I knew I was in for an unusual visit. He looked to be well into his teenage years, so it didn't surprise me to learn he was 16. The bigger surprise was that he was

Diary of a Mall Santa

serious about his visit. He wasn't there to taunt me, like so many other teenage boys.

Instead, he went immediately to the armrest and sat down. This gave me the impression he had rehearsed what he was about to say.

Charles was a good looking young man, and seemed like the kind of student who would excel in school.

"What are you thinking about for Christmas?" I asked.

"I want a car, Santa," he said matter-of-factly. Obviously, with a request like that, he wasn't going to bother me with incidental gift ideas.

"A car," I said, "Any particular make and model?" After all, he might as well be specific.

"I want a Mustang," he said, making direct eye contact with me. I glanced around to see if teenage friends were nearby. I might be getting set up for a master prank. I also had the feeling that his appeal for a car had fallen on deaf ears with his parents. I was his last resort.

So I continued. "Do you want a NEW Mustang?"

"Well, YEAH!" he said, as if my suggestion of a used Mustang was completely out of line.

I had to give the young man credit. What red-blooded 16-year-old boy wouldn't want a new Mustang? Yet I wasn't sure how to wrap this conversation up without giving in to his outrageous scheme.

"You look like a serious student," I said, "am I right?"

"Yes," he said as he nodded his head. "I make pretty good grades."

"Do you realize that the insurance premiums alone for new Mustang would make a big dent in your college tuition costs?"

He sat staring at me, and said nothing. I think he anticipated a big let down.

"I have a feeling you will do well in college too, and probably get a good job when you graduate. Maybe you need to postpone the new Mustang, and settle for something far less expensive." I felt like I was talking to one of my children when they were 16 and had similar dreams.

He finally smiled. "Yeah," he said, "that's what my dad said too."

We shook hands, and then he dashed off into his future.

Thankfully, the next child in line was only five years old. If he wants a Mustang, I thought to myself, it would be a Match Box model.

25 days before Christmas

LIVELY VISITORS, *11:11 a.m.*

I learned something new today. Some visitors think Santa is a chick magnet.

A lively family arrived just before noon. The group included five children, a father, and the children's aunt. They were a happy crew, primed and ready to party.

The children descended on Santa. Some on my lap, one on the arm of my chair, and one standing close by. The aunt, an attractive young woman with short wavy hair, wore a tight-fitting gray sweater. She sat on the other arm of my oversized chair. The man in the group, the children's father, stood several feet away, camera in hand.

My large red hat somehow got dislodged in the process, so the woman on the armrest retrieved it from the floor and placed it back on my head.

"Oh, look!" she said, "Santa has mistletoe on his hat."

I didn't correct her. The decoration was really plastic holly.

She hugged me tight around the neck with her bosom pressed against my face, and then firmly planted a kiss on my blushing red cheek.

I yielded to the raucous party atmosphere. Eventually the pictures were taken, gift requests were recorded, and the family waltzed out of Santa Land just as happy as when they had arrived.

෴

Diary of a Mall Santa

COZY COUPLE, *1:57 p.m.*

The young couple marched into Santa Land as if they were on a mission. Both wore wide grins. The woman was attractive with long, flowing dishwater blonde hair and form-fitting jeans. The man was a handsome, athletic-looking African-American, just slightly taller than his girlfriend. I stood to greet them. There were no other children or adults in line.

Before the couple reached my chair, the woman said, "We don't have any children yet. We just want to have our picture taken with you." I thought I detected a roguish look in her eyes.

"That can be arranged," I said. "Would you like to stand in front of the Christmas tree, with one of you on each side of me, and we can join in a group hug?"

Both moved right into position; the woman on my left and the man on my right. I put my outstretched arms around their shoulders, and my elf photographer stepped up to take the picture.

As I smiled at the camera, the woman softly placed her right hand directly on my rear end. I wondered – she couldn't possibly think that's my waist. I wore a 4" wide belt, and that was around my waist. Her hand was placed far below my belt. I still had trouble believing she intentionally placed her hand where it was.

I started to panic. What should I do?

I turned my head to the left and said, "That buttock belongs to Mrs. Santa and she is HOT." The smile quickly disappeared from her face and her hand moved away too.

൞

DRILL SERGEANT, *3:50 p.m.*

"Go see Santa. Sit down. Now smile. NOT LIKE THAT! Look at the camera. I SAID, LOOK AT THE CAMERA. What's wrong with you? Quit fidgeting. GET BACK ON SANTA'S LAP!"

Some parents barked out commands from the minute they entered Santa Land. It was usually an overbearing mother. The children were used to the badgering, and hardly ever responded as directed. They sat there with blank, sullen expressions. They showed no emotion. No joy, no sadness, no anger. Just vacant stares.

As a veteran father, my advice to anxious parents is this: just take the season in stride. Enjoy the moment. If your children don't smile broadly and gush with delight, just take the picture anyway. It's not that big of a deal. Smile and be kind to the children. A visit with Santa should be magical. Just allow the magic to happen and it will.

ଛେଓଃ

YOU AIN'T SITTIN' ON HIS LAP, 5:25 *pm.* Seasonal visits to see Santa have been an American tradition for generations. The routine is traditional too. Young children are eager to sit on Santa's lap, tell him how good they've been, and put in their requests for Christmas presents.

I have learned that there is something special about the Santa/child bond. Maybe sitting on the fat man's lap produces a sense of security. They can share their dreams with Santa on the comfort of his lap, and most children are not eager to leave. Santa is and should be accepting. He listens to their gift requests, but hears their stories too. Some stories are funny, some are heartbreaking, but most are fairly ordinary. Santa is not judgmental, but always loving and sensitive to their concerns and fears. Hollywood makes movies about bad Santas, but I can't believe there is any truth to the scripts. Any respectable shopping center would fire a bad Santa in a heartbeat.

That's why I was taken aback today when a father commanded his five-year-old son, "You ain't sittin' on his lap." He was serious. The son looked embarrassed. Perhaps he had seen his father's arrogant behavior before. He repeated himself, "YOU AIN'T SITTIN' ON HIS LAP."

I accepted the father's decree, but I was heartsick at his behavior.

The son stood several feet before me, looking awkward and humiliated, telling me his Christmas wishes. The interview ended quickly.

Perhaps the father thought I was a pervert. If there was a misguided soul in the room, it wasn't me.

Diary of a Mall Santa

I remember sitting on my father's lap when I was a child, and listening as he read the comic section of the newspaper. He used a different voice for each character. He would also read books as I followed along – learning to read in the process. It was a healthy, bonding father/son experience, and I followed his example when our children were young.

This story bothered me, not because of what the father said, but how his behavior will warp the values of his innocent young son. Just a reminder: parenting is the most sacred job we will ever have.

ೲ

24 days before Christmas

SANTA FEVER, *3:19 p.m.*

*S*ilvia had seen me earlier in the day, but she must have had Santa fever because she kept coming back with questions and requests.

She was tall and thin with long black hair and a ponytail. She had Hispanic features. Silvia was the picture of deportment. I could imagine her being a news anchor on television some day.

On her first return visit, she asked if I would wake her up when I arrived at her house on Christmas Eve, so she could serve me milk and cookies.

"I would love to, " I said, "but I have so many homes to visit I won't have any spare time."

"Then stop by my home last," she replied without pausing. It seemed like a perfect solution to her.

"I'm afraid I can't." I couldn't come up with a plausible excuse. Fortunately, her father called her away, and I was safe for the moment.

"I was wondering," she said on her return visit. She seemed to appear out of nowhere, like a stealth airplane. "Where do the reindeer stay during the day? Do they really like carrots?" She rattled off several questions about the reindeer, and I had no problem fabricating fictitious answers.

Once again her father called her back. She disappeared with a wave and a smile. On her third return visit, she asked, "Santa, may I ride in your sleigh on Christmas Eve?"

"It's so crowded with gifts, there's hardly room for a passenger. Besides, it's dangerous."

She was not about to lose another appeal. Luckily, a group of families entered Santa Land and my attention had to shift to the new visitors.

ಬಿಞ

EXPECTATIONS, *4:30 p.m.*

Jonah wore a brooding, dispassionate expression as he walked up to see me. I had seen this look too many times. I don't recall if a parent was nearby. He was heavy for a nine year old, and took up all the spare space in my chair. His hair was dark, and groomed to a peak in the middle, atop his head. He was not smiling, and I quickly learned why.

After the usual get acquainted banter, Jonah got to the real reason he had come to see me.

Stewart Scott

"Santa, what I really want for Christmas is for my parents to get back together," he said. He had turned his head toward me as he spoke.

I always ask God in prayer to provide wisdom and the words to comfort troubled children, but today I felt like I was totally on my own. I didn't know what to say.

Digging deep within myself, I told him, "Jonah, I'm so sorry," giving him a strong, one-armed hug. "Have you talked to your parents?"

"Yeah," he said, "and they said, 'It's not going to happen.' So I thought I would talk to you." No doubt his parents were going through pain and anger of their own. Perhaps they didn't realize how their broken marriage was affecting Jonah. For unknown reasons, there was no school counselor, pastor, priest or other trusted adult friend to whom he could talk. Both of us were misty eyed. So he put his trust in Santa, the go-to guy for childhood miracles. In his heart, he believed I could help.

"Jonah, I know your parents love you very much, and they both want to be part of your life."

Diary of a Mall Santa

Children walk in here with high expectations, but this request set the bar to a new level. I continue to pray for Jonah and his parents. God is bigger than anything we can hope or imagine. I guess I need to learn to trust God to assuage Jonah's pain, and continue to offer love and protection. Chances are I will never see Jonah again, and if I do, I won't be wearing a red suit.

Today's challenge reminded me of a long forgotten quote: "The boy who expects every morning to open into a new world finds that today is like yesterday, but he believes tomorrow will be different." Charles Warner

ಸಂಚ

STICK TO THE SUBJECT, *5:02 p.m.*

The child was formally dressed in a lavender outfit and she wore a stylish wool coat. Based on her appearance, I was sure she was here for a picture with Santa.

When the child sat on my lap, the mother declined the picture. "Some other time," she said.

I asked the child, "Where are you going, all dressed up like that?"

"Can we just talk about Christmas?" she replied.

I have the feeling she will make a fine prosecutor in about twenty years.

23 days before Christmas

SANTA IS FOR BELIEVERS, *3:14 p.m.*

Whenever I'm not listening to children's Christmas wishes or waiting for the next child to arrive, I'm searching the mall for believers. I try to attract everyone – old people, middle-aged people, teenagers and children. Most of all, children.

I usually say: "I'm so happy to see you here today." I try not to say: Come on in and see Santa,

Diary of a Mall Santa

unless they are already headed my way. I don't want to put the parents in an awkward position.

Santa is for children. I always want to have time for them, regardless of the situation. All too often, parents run out of time. Other priorities get in the way of listening and reacting to what is going on in their hearts and minds. My job is to listen and to offer encouragement.

When I'm walking through the mall, if I see children 50 feet away – I wave. If they run toward me with arms outstretched, I get down on their level and return their hugs. Santa can never be too busy to welcome children.

༄༅

MAGICAL MOMENT, *4:45 p.m.*

A bashful five-year-old girl slowly approached me today. She was a slender little girl, with tightly woven braids and colorful beads in her hair. Someone spent hours preparing her hair, probably her mother. As she got closer to my Santa chair, with me scooted forward on the cushion, her otherwise pretty face took on a look of abject terror.

"I know, I know," I told the parents. "Sometimes I even scare myself. When I look at my face in the mirror in the morning, I say 'YIKES!'"

The parents laughed.

I held out the mall coloring book to take the little girl's attention of off my daunting red outfit. When she took hold of the book, I slowly pulled the book (and the girl) toward me, like a fisherman reeling in his catch. Before we knew it, she was right in front of me and I motioned for her to turn around so I could lift her onto my lap. The technique worked like charm.

Once on my lap, we began our chat, and her look of terror disappeared. She was caught up in the magical moment and enjoyed her visit with Santa. So did I.

The parents said that was the first time their daughter ever sat on Santa's lap.

Diary of a Mall Santa

ANOTHER FIRST, *5:30 p.m.*

Once again, my constant waving, ringing of sleigh bells, and greeting mall customers paid off.

A woman cautiously entered my Santa domain today. She was stylishly dressed like a professional who had just come from work. I think my energetic waving had attracted her. She mentioned that she was 59 years old and had never visited Santa before, even as a child. A disarming, expectant smile graced her beaming face.

"Let's fix that right now," I said. "Would you like to have your picture taken in front of the Christmas tree or with me on my chair?"

"I want to sit on your lap," she said, without pausing. "I've never done that before."

Her visit with Santa blessed her day, and blessed mine too.

I later learned that she had just lost her husband. She promised to return with her eight grandchildren for a family picture.

ಸಂಡ

Stewart Scott

FRIENDS VISIT, *6:13 p.m.*

Jennifer and Don, two good friends, visited today with their three young daughters. The parents knew who was behind the Santa beard, but their children had no idea.

The children were ecstatic. They rushed me with open arms, hollering, "Santa! Santa!"

"Do you know who that is?" asked the mother. The children ignored her question. To them I was simply Santa.

I greeted each child by name.

The flood of warmth from those beautiful children was amplified by the beaming smiles on the parents' faces. They were caught up in the moment too, just like their children.

ಸಾಡ

Diary of a Mall Santa

22 days before Christmas

BASS BOAT DAVE, *4:09 p.m.*

*D*ave was a brash former Navy boatswain's mate, in his 50s or early 60s, with a stubble beard and a rugged face. He proudly wore a ball cap bearing the name of one of the destroyers he had served aboard.

Dave met me at the exit door to Santa Land; I don't think he actually intended to approach me in my comfortable Santa chair with his Christmas wish list.

I started the conversation. "You must be a Navy vet," I inquired. "Is that the ship you served aboard?" I asked, pointing to his hat.

That's all I needed to say to launch Dave into a detailed description of his colorful 18-year Navy career. He was proud to be a boatswain's mate. They're the tough guys aboard ship. On 100-degree days, the boatswain's mates are chipping rusted paint; and on sub-freezing days, they're the sailors heaving heavy lines ashore. They wear their tattoos proudly; they drink more and party harder than most of the other sailors.

Dave was glad to share sea stories with Santa, but he really wanted to tell me about his Christmas wish list.

"Santa, you know that boat store on Cicero Avenue just north of here?" he asked. He went on to tell me about the variety of boats they have on display. "I want that 18-foot bass boat." His eyes revealed his passion for fishing and his desire for that sleek bass boat of his dreams.

"Yes, I know exactly where it is," I said. "Sounds like you really want that boat. Sounds like a cool idea."

I steered the conversation toward Dave's Navy career and allowed him to regale me with salty stories of days gone by. He took the bait. Sailors love to share sea stories.

Dave asked, "Do you know the difference between a sea story and a fairytale?"

"No," I said, and waited for the punch line.

"Fairytales begin with 'Once upon a time,' " he said, "and sea stories start with, 'this ain't no shit.' "

We both laughed.

Dave didn't want to end our conversation without bringing up the bass boat again. He was serious about the gift. Sharing sea stories was fun, but he was there to see Santa for one reason: the bass boat.

"When you head north on Cicero," he continued, "you'll want to turn left on 151st Street." He proceeded to provide specific directions to his house, turn by turn, with all the landmarks of service stations and convenience stores along the way.

I knew exactly what he was doing. He wanted to make sure the bass boat arrived by Christmas morning.

"Wait a minute," I added. "I don't think that boat will fit in my sleigh."

"You got a trailer hitch, don't you?" he said without a pause or a smile.

"They told me two things when I took this job," I said. "Keep both hands visible at all times and don't promise anybody anything."

That brought Dave back to earth. Perhaps he headed over to another shopping center to con their Santa out of his coveted bass boat.

༺༻

THE BEST GIFT OF ALL, *5:23 p.m.*

Stacy and her parents returned today, and they brought cousins along this time. I met Stacy the first or second day on the job.

Stacy was a sophomore in high school, but she believed in Santa with the faith of a child. Her face seemed to have a permanent, radiant smile; her light-brown hair was pulled back in a ponytail. She knew each reindeer by name. I made up stories about the quirks of each reindeer, and Stacy listened with interest. I told her how stubborn Donner is and how Comet always goes too fast, forcing me to slow him down. Santa can get by with outrageous stories.

Stacy's father was out of a job. The only thing she asked me for was a job for her dad. I wished I could somehow make that dream come true. Stacy and her mom asked me to pray for their family, right in the heart of Santa Land.

☙❧

SIDEBAR STORY, *6:05 p.m.*

The day-to-day Santa operation is run like a business. Photos with Santa generate income for the mall. When the color printers get low on ink, one of the elves calls Security on a walkie-talkie to request more ink cartridges. The conversation is short and to the point: "Santa to Security. Please bring us more ink cartridges. We're getting low."

Security quickly responds with an abrupt, "10-4."

We know that "10-4" means they heard our request, but it doesn't necessarily mean they're going to do anything about it. If we don't have ink by the following morning, we call Security again. Their response is the same: "10-4." It's an on-going problem. Not only does it frustrate customers when we can't take pictures, it also means less income for the mall.

Stewart Scott

We rarely see Security, even when teenagers are racing through mall with their jeans hanging down below their butts. Moreover, that kind of behavior doesn't endear paying customers to the mall at a time when most businesses are still reeling from the poor economy.

But we managed to solve the ink problem without even trying. Here's what happened.

Several weeks into the season, the mall hired a new elf. Laurie was a 19-year-old college freshman and very attractive. She also felt it would enhance her elf image if she wore tight red or green leotards, along with tight, colorful sweaters. Her blonde hair, blue eyes and warm, personable smile completed the ensemble.

During her second day in Santa Land, one of the younger security guards became a permanent addition. If Laurie was there, so was the security guard. Perhaps he thought it was his job to protect her against unruly customers. He frequently chatted with Laurie, yet I think he was more interested in seeing her later in the day – after work. Laurie didn't seem to mind the attention.

During a slow period, I approached the security guard to thank him for his special interest in the Santa operation. He responded by saying he was there because of the large amount of cash we had in the register. Sure.

The good news is: whenever Laurie worked, we never ran out on ink.

൭൨

WORLD PEACE, *6:05 p.m.*

Many children asked for a litany of expensive gifts, and I stoically tolerated their requests. But when nine-year-old Melinda asked for world peace, it jolted me for a moment. I wasn't expecting that.

"How do you think we can achieve world peace?" I asked, trying to involve her in the process. "What do you think we can do?"

She was ready with an answer. She was a smart little girl. She had thought through this procedure more than I realized.

Stewart Scott

"I think you need to visit every house in the world and talk to the people about world peace. Tell them how devastating war is. It's so unnecessary. I'm sure they will listen to you."

I felt duped. Why is it my job? Don't I do enough by delivering gifts to children everywhere? You have no idea how exhausted I am by Christmas morning.

Melinda is a budding politician, I thought. She'll come up with the ideas, but someone else has to do the heavy lifting.

ಸಂಬಂ

Diary of a Mall Santa

FIRST INTERMEZZO

THE STORY OF SAINT NICHOLAS

Santa Claus, the jolly old man with a fat little tummy, has been secularized over the centuries. Today he is synonymous with gift giving. Gift giving did not start with the biblical accounts of the arrival of Jesus, whose birthday we celebrate on Christmas Day.

Nicholas was born into a wealthy Greek family in the latter part of the third century. Christians were persecuted at that time, yet his parents raised him in the Christian faith. Chances are he was lean and trim –not overweight. Historians seem to agree that he did have a white beard though.

When Nicholas was a young man, his parents died from an epidemic, and he inherited great wealth. Nicholas obeyed the biblical admonition to "Sell what you have and give your money to the poor." He was made Bishop of Myra (now part of Turkey), and became known throughout the land for his generosity to the poor, especially to children and others in need.

One story related how Nicholas had helped a poor woman who required a dowry if she was to marry. On three separate evenings, stockings filled with gold balls were tossed through the family's window; the gold became her dowry, and made it possible for her to marry well, and avoid being sold into slavery. That ancient custom gave birth to Christmas stockings being hung by the chimney. Today, oranges are often placed in Christmas stockings on the night before Christmas; the oranges symbolize the gold balls, according to legend.

Nicholas died on December 6, 343 A.D., and that day is recognized as Saint Nicholas Day. (December 19 according to the Julian calendar.) In parts of Europe, that is the primary day of gift giving – not Christmas Day, (December 25).

The church canonized him about one hundred years after his death, and Catholics, the Orthodox Church, and Protestants all recognize his sainthood today.

Diary of a Mall Santa

Wouldn't it be nice if we could follow the example of Saint Nicholas next Christmas, and give to the less fortunate? Such people are all around us, if we watch for them through the eyes of Santa.

Stewart Scott

21 days before Christmas

NICE MOHAWK, *3:19 p.m.*

"Cool haircut!" I said, when a little five-year-old boy arrived with a Mohawk. The narrow band of black hair was spiked and groomed to perfection.

The mother announced that they had just come from the barber.

I quietly reflected: I wish now that I had said, "Cool haircut" when my son Andy came home one day years ago with his own Mohawk. He was in his early teens at the time, and starting to distance himself from his parents. Instead of making a favorable comment, I expressed my displeasure.

Wisdom and tolerance come with age and experience. Fathers, learn from my mistake. It's only hair. It will grow back.

ಸಂಬ

Diary of a Mall Santa

QUE DIOS TE BENDIGA, *3:50 p.m.*

About twenty percent of the children who visited me were Hispanic. While the kids spoke English, often the parents continued to speak in their native language.

I wanted to find a way to reach these children in Spanish, yet I hoped to go beyond the traditional greetings of "Buenos Dias" or "Feliz Navidad."

So I asked my friend Yolanda, a native of Peru, "How do you say 'God bless you' in Spanish?" I thought this phrase would be a nice way to end conversations with Latino children, and send them off feeling "blessed" by the experience.

"Que Dios te bendiga," she said, and then coached me in the proper pronunciation.

My noble plan backfired.

An Hispanic family brought their seven-year-old daughter to see me. In the course of our conversation, I asked the little girl, "Habla Español?"

"Yes," she said in English.

"Que Dios te bendiga," I said. "Do you know what that means?"

"Merry Christmas?" she asked, looking a little unsure of herself.

Either my pronunciation was very bad or the little girl didn't speak Spanish as well as I imagined.

Que sera.

ಶಂಡ

THE ABC SONG, *4:12 p.m.*

It didn't take long to learn that children between one year and two-and-a-half years old are likely to be terrified of Santa. Unfortunately, it's hard for me to pacify their fears because Santa is the source of their fear.

Parents, on the other hand, have planned the visit carefully. Often the child is neatly dressed for a photo with Santa. So when children dig their heels in and scream bloody murder, the parents are even more determined. They demand compliance. They command a serene smile. Sometimes they shout out their orders like an angry football coach on the sidelines. Yet the children continue to scream.

Diary of a Mall Santa

Older children see a loving, grandfatherly Santa. Younger children see a strange man wearing a disguise.

Once a child arrives on my lap, frantically trying to escape, I discovered that if I softly sing the ABC song he or she will often relax. It's magical. They hear a familiar song, and sometimes will even sing along with me. But just because children stop screaming, it doesn't mean they will smile like a winning candidate on election night. The parents aren't content with a quiet child. They also demand a perfect smile. You can't win.

Hallmark moments are hard to come by.

ೋಡ

WOMAN WANTS WINDFALL, *6:36 p.m.*

Once again, near the end of my four-hour shift, I strolled into the mall to greet customers and recruit children for visits with Santa.

An older couple was slowly walking past rows of stores, and I waved and greeted the woman who was several paces behind her husband.

"What you gonna bring me for Christmas this year, Santa?" she said in a loud, demanding voice.

"One of my elves told me you wanted a new Lexus," I quickly answered.

"BALONEY," she replied. "I want the winning numbers for the lottery. Besides, I have a perfectly good Ford that runs just fine." She was serious.

All I could do was laugh. She left me at a loss for words. Besides, if I could produce the winning lottery numbers, I would start playing the game myself, cash in, and retire.

But I wouldn't give up my Santa job.

೧೧

KATIE AND THE SLEIGH BELLS, *7:15 p.m.*

At the end of my shift, a woman approached me with her adult child. Katie was 20 years old, tall and thin, with short black hair. Her mother quietly told me she was a special needs child. Katie not only still believed in Santa, but she knew each reindeer by name.

She had an affliction that caused jerking movements, similar to the symptoms of Parkinson's disease, so I tried hard to make her feel comfortable. I spoke softly and gave her my full attention.

Katie spotted my sleigh bells and took an immediate interest. "When I ring the bells," I told her, "the reindeer come running, so we better not ring the bells too loudly." She was fascinated by them. She held them tight as she studied each bell and gently shook them.

The mother intervened. "Katie," she said, "give Santa his sleigh bells. He needs to go now."

The mother seemed to know that my shift had ended 15 minutes earlier.

In retrospect, I wish I had given her the sleigh bells. The simple gift would have meant so much to that beautiful adult child.

Stewart Scott

20 days before Christmas

SANTA IS RECRUITED, *12:15 p.m.*

*M*ost people waved back when I greeted them in the mall. Old people, young people, children, teenagers – almost everyone smiled and waved back. Except for teenage boys. The boys often had an abundance of gold jewelry around their necks and facial piercings, and their trousers were slung low, exposing their boxer underwear and other parts of their anatomy.

Rather than wave, they would flash me a horizontal "V" formed with the middle and index fingers of one hand. It looked a little like a sideways peace symbol, and the sign was often concealed close to their bodies – not to be seen by too many people. It was a quick sign, and one they had practiced many times. A smile didn't accompany the sign, but sometimes they would say, "Whazzup!"

Diary of a Mall Santa

I'm not a real street-savvy Santa. Do you think it's a gang sign and they're trying to recruit me?

※

GRAMMAR LESSON, *1:35 p.m.*

Butchered English grammar bothered me, and a large percentage of the children who visited me were guilty. Sometimes I felt like it was my duty to correct poor grammar, but I usually resisted the temptation. After all, that job belonged to parents and teachers. But who was going to hire a young man or woman 15 years from now if they couldn't speak reasonably correct English? So, maybe it was my public duty to do something now.

Today a nine-year-old boy with a gloomy expression joined me for a conversation. Before I could ask him what he wanted for Christmas, he anticipated my question and said, "Grandma says we ain't gettin' nothin' this year."

"YOU ARE NOT GETTING ANYTHING THIS YEAR," I said, trying to correct his slang.

With that the boy burst into tears, twisted himself free from my lap, and ran out of Santa Land.

Maybe my grammar lesson wasn't the best idea after all.

ಬಿಂಬ

A GIFT FOR SANTA, *2:17 p.m.*

Mandy made my day when she marched right up and handed me a gift. She gave me a paperweight filled with artificial snow and a winter scene inside. When you turned it upside down, the snow slowly floated to the base. She also gave me several pages from her coloring book, neatly colored.

I heard a lot of requests for gifts from children. So this was an unanticipated, refreshing present.

Mandy, I will always keep that paperweight and think of you whenever I see it.

ಬಿಂಬ

SUNDAE SPECIAL, *2:42 p.m.*

Santa was faced with a few pesky obstacles every day. They came in all shapes, sizes and situations.

Diary of a Mall Santa

Today's first obstacle, a stout seven-year-old lad, arrived holding a giant chocolate marshmallow sundae with whipped cream and a cherry on top. A third of the monstrous concoction was spread across his face; another third was dripping down the sleeves of his black leather jacket. I quickly insisted that the dessert be left in the care of his mother while we visited and posed for a picture.

If his mother had used her moistened fingers to clean his face, she could have made a complete meal of it.

As luck would have it, I had taken my Santa suit home for dry cleaning the night before, and hoped I could protect it for the remainder of the season.

As the boy climbed up on my lap, I watched him carefully, paying special attention to the ice cream covering his face and the snaking drips of chocolate and marshmallow sauce on his sleeves. I tried to hold him in such a way that my clean suit would be protected. It wasn't easy.

It was difficult to watch his every move and listen with rapt attention to his gift requests at the same time. Without warning, he slipped off my lap and collapsed in a bundle on the carpeted floor. Fearing he had hit a chocolate sauce slick, I searched my suit for telltale signs.

It took a few moments, but he eventually regained his composure and returned to his waiting mother. His arms were outstretched to reclaim his delicious sundae.

ଈଔ

BILINGUAL SANTA, *3:10 p.m.*

An Hispanic family came to see me with four bright-eyed children. When they hopped on my lap, the mother gave them instructions in Spanish. "Aqui, aqui," she said, as she told them where to stand or sit.

I knew I had an authentic Mexican family so I was determined to try my new Spanish phrase again. I hoped for more success this time.

"Que Dios te bendiga," I whispered to one little girl with dark eyes and short black hair.

She nodded her head and asked, "Como se llama?"

Diary of a Mall Santa

"Santa, me llama es Santa," I said, in my precarious high school Spanish

For a bright and shining moment, I felt totally bilingual.

Feliz Navidad!

ಐಖ

19 days before Christmas

SLIP OF THE TONGUE, *1:10 p.m.*
If this encounter with young Kevin sounds similar to other stories, it's because tales about terrified children always captured my full attention, and they happened more frequently than you might imagine.

From the moment the boy was tugged kicking and screaming into Santa Land, I knew big trouble was headed my way. He had made up his mind that a visit with Santa was not on his agenda, and his father hadn't received the memo.

Stewart Scott

Dad took control, only because he was bigger and stronger. He lifted Kevin by one wrist and held the quivering child at arm's length. He clearly did not want to feel the effect of the boy's flailing feet armed with heavy winter boots.

When Kevin landed in a heap on my lap, he didn't stop resisting. He twisted, turned, gyrated and jerked, like a spastic break-dancer. I tried to calm him and control his wild movements. I don't think I could have restrained him if I had managed to wrestle him into a full nelson. So I let him slide quickly and ungracefully into a pile of convulsing arms and legs on the carpeted floor.

The father was taken aback. I saw it in his eyes. Isn't Santa supposed to have magical powers over uncontrollable children?

In my frustrated state I blurted out, "I cannot have a child jerking off on my lap." (Silence) I meant to say – I cannot restrain a child against his will. I realized my mistake the moment I uttered the fatal words.

Diary of a Mall Santa

I wondered what the father told his wife at the dinner table that evening about Kevin's visit with Santa.

☙❧

MACARONI AND CHEESE, *2:20 p.m.*

Lyle was only three, yet his mother expected him to smile broadly for the perfect holiday picture. Coaxing a smile out of the boy was going to be impossible, but I had to go along with the routine. Mothers and fathers made silly faces, offered bribes – then threats, and furiously shook jingle bells in a futile attempt to produce one simple smile.

I tried to help too, but my influence was limited – or ignored. Children didn't smile just because the request came from Santa.

As parents yelled "cheese," the star struck children still maintained the same stoic expressions.

With the camera poised, waiting for the perfect smile, I introduced a new twist on the "cheese" command, and said, "MACARONI AND CHEESE!"

My comment must have struck Lyle's funny bone, and he convulsed in laughter. Almost instantly, his mother ran forward and SMACK! – She slapped him silly. "Don't act like that," she said, "we're trying to get a smile out of you."

Then the mother said, "I give up."

A vicious slap in the face was more likely to produce a DCFS case worker than a smile.

You will read several stories about the quests for perfect smiles. This is a common theme in Santa Land, and it surfaces almost every day, yet the content is always different.

ಐಡಿ

18 days before Christmas

MISCHIEVOUS ELVES, 6:02 *a.m.*

Right after the alarm sounded at 6 this morning, Jean said, "I got up in the middle of the night, and there was a giant piece of French toast in our front yard."

"It sounds like the work of one of my elves," I said, without lifting my head from the pillow.

When I retrieved the newspaper about 6:30, there was indeed a large piece of French toast in the front yard. I suspected a frightened raccoon had dropped it. My elves have better manners.

I love this job, but the Santa persona is beginning to control my life.

෴

ACTION FIGURES, *3:41 p.m.*

It pleased me that little boys were still asking for action figures. Superman and Spiderman were the most popular. Action figures were three-dimensional, and they inspired creativity and stimulated the child's imagination – something video games do not, at least in my opinion.

There was a harmless game I played with children who asked for action figures. If a little boy (and it usually was little boys) asked for Superman, I would say, "Who's stronger, Spiderman or Superman?"

They responded with confidence, "Superman is!"

Then I would ask, "Who's stronger, Superman or Santa Claus?"

There was always a pause. If they said, "Superman," they thought they might risk getting gifts on Christmas morning.

If they said, "Santa Claus is the strongest!" (and some of them did), they were playing to my ego and guaranteeing their wish list would be fulfilled.

I thanked them for their high opinion of me, but reminded them that I was not nearly as strong as Superman. Spiderman was a different story.

ෂාஐ

DON'T READ ON A FULL STOMACH, *4:08 p.m.*

Several weeks before my first Santa appearance, I stopped at the mall deli for a corned beef sandwich on rye. The owner was a generously proportioned woman, and she casually wiped her grimy hands on her apron before she prepared my lunch. I think I saw traces of mustard on her fingers – at least I hoped it was mustard. When I noticed the lack of rubber gloves, I inwardly began to question the hygiene standards of her restaurant.

In the course of our conversation, I told her about my Santa job. She smiled broadly and promised to bring her children in for a visit.

When the group arrived about 10 days later, the three children, two girls and one boy, were dressed in soiled, wrinkled clothing, and had tussled dirty hair and stains of chocolate ice cream on their ruddy faces – probably left over from the night before.

As they began to gather near my chair, I contemplated the quality of the picture they would receive. Would any of the dirt and grime transfer to my snow-white beard?

The mom swept her hands across the children's heads, one by one, to add some semblance of decorum to their unruly hair. Then, using her pinky finger, she plucked boogers from their nostrils and wiped the remnants on her tattered jeans. She wet her thumb on her outstretched tongue and began wiping away the chocolate stains and mucus from their upper lips – and repeated the process over and over until the children were more presentable. They cooperated fully, as if this was a household ritual.

My stomach began to rumble. It was not a good feeling. If cookies and milk are waiting for me on Christmas Eve, I think I'll pass them by.

ಸಂಬ

16 days before Christmas*

HUGE CHILDREN, *1:18 p.m.*

I have noticed a direct correlation between the weight of a child and his or her strong desire for a long list of electronic games. The children who asked for baseball gloves and soccer balls tended to be much trimmer. Some of the boys and girls were so heavy, I had to ask one of the elves to help hoist the child onto my lap. When I was a child, I lived on Ho-Hos, Ding-

Diary of a Mall Santa

Dongs and Hostess Cup Cakes. When I wasn't pigging out on sweets, I was playing baseball, football, or basketball. When I was 16, I weighted 145 pounds and was six feet tall. No matter how much food I consumed, I couldn't add a single pound. My only electronic addiction was the Howdy Doody show.

There must be a lesson in this observation. Rather than place surtaxes on junk foods or make them illegal, maybe we should apply enormous taxes to electronic games, making them too expensive to buy.

ಬಂ

UNIVERSAL LOVE, *2:03 p.m.*

Just as one family was leaving after a pleasant visit, two children ran toward me, arms outstretched, shouting, "Santa, Santa." Within a nanosecond, we were engulfed in a loving hug. One child quickly climbed up on my right knee while his sister, about seven years old, snuggled between me and the armrest of my chair. They couldn't wait to ask about the reindeer, Mrs. Santa and the elves. Moments like these are why I love being Santa.

The family was African-American. Mom and Dad looked on adoringly at their enthusiastic children, both with broad smiles. This visit was all they expected it to be – an opportunity for their children to be loved and listened to by Santa. It was an integral part of their Christmas experience.

It occurred to me, there was no prejudice where Santa was concerned. It didn't make any difference to the parents or the children if I was white, black, Asian or from any other ethnic or racial group. Santa Claus was universally loved because he represented generosity and unconditional love. Skin color had nothing to do with it.

ೞದ

WANTS MOM FOR CHRISTMAS, *2:25 p.m.*

A sweet nine-year-year old girl visited me today. Her name was Gracie. She had delicate features, short blonde hair and just the hint of a smile.

Diary of a Mall Santa

She relished her time with Santa and seemed to want to linger even after I listened to her Christmas wishes.

I asked, "Is there anything else you would like to talk to Santa about?"

"Would you ask my mom to visit me for Christmas?" she said.

Her father stood less than 10 feet away with a stern expression on his face. He heard his daughter's plea. "Tell her she doesn't need her mother," he said. "I can be both."

"It sounds like you really miss your mom," I said, then allowed her to return to her frowning father.

If you would like all of the stories in this diary to be funny and entertaining, so do I -- but that's not the real world.

ಬಂಡ

MELTDOWN, *3:05 p.m.*

I came close to a meltdown today. A family took over Santa Land for at least 15 minutes. Fortunately, other children weren't waiting in line.

Stewart Scott

The mother was clearly in charge of her brood. Her figure looked like an inverted equilateral triangle. She had broad shoulders and a wholesome bosom, and her figure tapered down from there. She talked and barked out commands incessantly, like an adult who needed a double dose of Ritalin®. While the mom darted after Rocky and Nicky, her two young children, the father snapped off picture after picture on his expensive Nikon.

Her objective was to get the youngsters on my lap and have them pose gracefully for the camera. It was not to be. Each boy scampered around Santa Land like a running back heading for the end zone.

The mother's commands fell on deaf ears. Her boys were not about to cooperate.

Finally, Mom resorted to bribery. She gave each boy a container of treats. They might have been Cracker Jacks. Each child stuffed treats in his gaping mouth and dropped just as many morsels in his wake. Mom followed them around picking up the discards. Her bribes were not about to coax good behavior out of her children. They never arrived safely on my lap. If she had dropped her children on my lap, I would have had to let them slither to the floor still kicking and screaming.

Junk food bribes don't seem to be a good way to persuade children to behave like mature adults. Take a hint from Pavlov. His dog salivated every time he heard a bell ring. Her children were learning that they will be rewarded with delicious treats when they act up.

ഩരാ

15 days before Christmas

JUST SPANK ME, *1:58 p.m.*

A young couple arrived to see me today; they entered through the exit door. Both were in their late teens. The girl had shoulder-length, reddish-blonde hair, a light complexion with a scattering of freckles, and stylish designer glasses with black frames. Her boyfriend wore a silly grin. I suspected mischief.

Doug, one of my elves, asked, "Would you like to have your picture taken with Santa?"

"Yes," the girl said, "but we want to do something different."

"Be creative," I said. "What would you like to do?"

I could almost see the wheels turning in her pretty head. I knew she came prepared with an unusual idea.

"Could we take the picture with Santa slapping my ass?" she asked, without an ounce of modesty.

I wondered – if we had a video camera, I could keep on spanking away for at least five minutes. The clip would go viral on Youtube and I would be famous -- and unemployed. No, I thought, I like this job too much to get myself fired.

They opted for a conventional group-hug picture with Santa in front of the Christmas tree. They left a little disappointed.

ಸಂಡ

Diary of a Mall Santa

THE POOPING DOLL, *2:19 p.m.*

There were trends in what children asked for each Christmas. Popular items for the season this year were Barbie dolls and video games. But today I heard a new request.

"I want a doll that poops in her pants," a six-year-old girl asked.

I didn't know they made such things. I learned later that some enterprising toy manufacturer does indeed make dolls that poop in their pants. I wondered if the dolls had some kind of shunt near their belly buttons, and if the gift came with a bag of synthetic poop.

"I'll see what I can do," I said, "My elves are pretty resourceful. And they're really good at making Barbie dolls."

I sure hope that little girl isn't let down on Christmas morning.

ഐര

Stewart Scott

SHE STILL BELIEVES, *3:05 p.m.*

A young woman in her late twenties kept glancing at me today. The first time I saw her she was on the escalator. I spotted her again about five minutes later standing near the exit to Santa Land.

I waved HELLO and said that I was glad she was here. "I was hoping you would come see me," I added, as I walked up to meet her. I assumed everyone was a fan of Santa, not just children.

Sensing the look of concern in her eyes, I reached out to hold both of her hands, and said, "Hi. How are you? I'm glad you came to see me."

"Santa, will you pray for me?" she asked anxiously.

"Yes, of course," I said. "HOW can I pray for you?"

She told me her name was Jeannie and she had a swollen lymph gland in her neck. She was obviously upset. She told me she was going to see the doctor soon.

I am overwhelmed that God would send Jeannie to me, and ask for prayers.

Diary of a Mall Santa

Albert Einstein once said, "Coincidence is God working anonymously."

☙❧

ARE YOU SANTA? *7:25 p.m.*

As I retreated to my dressing room at the end of a tiring shift, I noticed two girls – about 10 years old – sitting on a bench. I waved my customary greeting, and went through the hidden passageways to enter the back door of my dressing room.

A half hour or more passed before I was dressed in street clothes again and ready to take the long walk through the mall and back to my car.

The girls were still seated on the bench when I left, and one of them asked, "Are you Santa?"

"What?" I said. "What did you say?" acting somewhat astonished.

They said nothing. I think my cover was safe for another day.

☙❧

Stewart Scott

SECOND INTERMEZZO

The 10 things I've learned while being Santa

Several of these suggestions are repeated
in stories throughout the diary.

1. NO COUNTER STORIES

*I*n casual conversations we tell "counter stories." For example, if a friend tells you they just got over a cold, you will probably tell him about an ailment of your own. That's a counter story. Counter stories propel most conversations.

Santa can't tell counter stories. Santa asks questions, listens and asks more questions.

It would be out of character to tell a child about my children and their experiences. In their minds there is just Santa, Mrs. Santa, the reindeer and the elves. My credibility would vanish if they knew I was a mortal father of five.

2. ENCOURAGE CHILDREN

Without consciously meaning to, some parents condemn their children, not their children's behavior.

If you constantly tell your child he is bad, he will live up to your expectations.

Many parents have scolded their children in front of me. "Tell Eddie he is bad," they would say, "and if he doesn't behave, you won't bring him anything for Christmas." In the meantime, the dejected child just cowers before me, imagining a barren spot beneath the Christmas tree where his presents should be waiting. What a harsh thought.

So, I tell children, "When I look into your eyes, I see a good little boy (or girl). Santa loves you." Parents can do the same. You have your children all year long. I just see them in December.

Christmas may not last all year-round, but children should believe that parental love is without limits.

3. TEENAGERS AREN'T SO BAD

The woman who coached me before my Santa assignment warned me about teenagers. I was a little concerned. What if a group of rowdy kids tried to pull off my beard?

However, when a group of three teenage girls shyly walked into Santa Land, I knew they had not totally abandoned their belief in Santa. They wanted to relive the wonder of their childhoods, and I wanted to encourage their dreams.

A lot of adults hold on to their childhood fantasies, and why should we discourage that? If Santa represents goodness, love, and generosity, those aren't bad attributes to embrace.

4. WELCOME EVERYONE

When I embarked on my assignment, I thought Santa was just for children.

That's not true. Santa is universally adored. I greet everyone, regardless of age. My experiences are filled with stories of adults who still need what Santa represents. I only hope I was able to fulfill their expectations.

5. ALWAYS BE IN CHARACTER

From the moment I walk out of my dressing room until the time I return, I am Santa to the people who see me. I am not a director or a manager. It is not my job to scold children or control the long line of eager kids waiting to see me. I am not the photographer or even the photo director. I am strictly Santa; that is my character.

I am there for the children and other believers. My job is to listen, to care, and to dole out hugs generously.

Sidebar: I wish I had the positive, saint-like attributes of the original Saint Nicholas, but in real life I fall far short. I'm playing a role, like an actor, and trying to do it well.

6. HOW TO CALM A TERRORIZED CHILD, PART ONE

As a father, I've learned how to gently calm distressed children. But when Santa is the source of their terror, there is little I can do. You can't imagine the horrified look in a child's eyes when they see Santa for the first time.

Here's one more trick. When a terrorized child arrives to see me, the first thing I do is turn him toward the camera – and away from me. There is something about the beard and red suit that sends him into orbit. Then, if the child is still crying and twisting to free himself from my arms, I gently sing a familiar song, like the childhood ABC song. In most cases the child quickly calms down. He hears a well-known melody, and sometimes starts to sing along with me. The parents get on board too. "Yes, Timmy, you know that song."

With apologies to Shakespeare, I can safely say, "Music calms the savage toddler."

7. HOW TO CALM A TERRORIZED CHILD, PART TWO

Here's another idea. I'll take the credit for discovering this technique on my own.

When the child is standing about five feet from me, and won't step forward another inch, I hold out our mall coloring book for her to study. The pictures of Santa and the reindeer immediately catch her eye. In most cases, the child will reach for the book, expecting me to let go. I don't. Rather, I use the book to pull the child toward me. Once she is standing before me, I motion for her to turn around (to face the opposite direction), and lift her onto my lap.

The success rate isn't 100%, but for you aspiring Santas out there, it's worth a try.

8. COMMUNICATE WITH PARENTS

If a child demonstrates a positive quality, tell the parents. This reinforces constructive behaviors.

For example, out of the hundreds of children who visited me at the mall, only one child asked for

Lincoln Logs. I heard plenty of appeals for expensive electronic games.

I told the parents, "Bobby is the only child so far to ask for Lincoln Logs. He must be very creative."

"Oh, he wants MORE Lincoln Logs?" the mother said, with an exasperated look on her face.

There are many such opportunities to accentuate positive attributes. Tell the children and pass the praise on to parents. Parenting is a difficult job, and encouraging feedback is hard to come by.

9. SANTA MEANS SAINT

People often need to be reminded that Santa is the Italian and Spanish word for saint. By most definitions, a saint is a superlatively good person.

The word "saint" comes from the Latin word "Sanctus," or sanctified.

When you put on the Santa suit, you become a saint in the eyes of the children. Always try to live up to their expectations.

Diary of a Mall Santa

10. LOVE CHILDREN

If you are inclined to call children "rug rats," don't apply for a Santa Claus job.

    Santa Claus has to love children. Modern-day Santas should follow the example of the original Saint Nicholas. Don't mess things up.

    You can't pretend to love children. You really have to care if you are going to be their super hero for the season.

Stewart Scott

14 days before Christmas

PARENTING, *11:27 a.m.*

A couple dressed their two-year-old daughter for a photo with me. She wore a flowing black dress with a decorative red bow and black patent leather shoes with leather soles. She had a pleasant expression on her face, until her eyes met mine. From the expectant look in the parents' eyes, they were probably envisioning a darling shot – a suitable enclosure for their seasonal Christmas card.

The daughter had other plans.

The mother was determined, and the father stood by with his camera, snapping off shot after shot.

As Mom marched her daughter to Santa, the little girl quickly dug in her heels and shrieked with fear. I held out my arms to welcome her, but from the expression on her face she looked like she was gazing into the hideous countenance of Satan. Didn't he wear a red suit too? As her mouth contorted and tears sprayed from her eyes, Mom lifted her daughter by one wrist with a strong, out-stretched arm. The child screamed as her legs kicked in all directions, and the one free arm flailed about like a windmill in a hurricane. That didn't deter the mom. She was determined to get the perfect picture, regardless of the emotional damage to the child or physical harm to Santa.

Mom dropped her hysterical daughter in my lap, still kicking and screaming, then did an abrupt about-face and marched back to her husband. I'm sure she expected that her daughter would immediately transform into a compliant child and flash a smile like Julia Roberts at the Oscars.

As those kicking hard-soled shoes came closer to my lap, I began to fear for my safety.

So, I gracefully let the crazed child slide from my lap to the floor. The mother wasn't happy. After all, she had spent hours preparing her daughter for the big event.

"I can't restrain a child against her will," I said. I wanted to make sure I didn't say something inappropriate, like I did in the story entitled, "Slip of the Tongue."

The mother grabbed her daughter, again by the wrist, and ushered her out of Santa Land with a huff. The family didn't return for an encore.

When parents presented me with an hysterical child who clearly was not ready for the Santa experience, I advised them to take a short break, do some shopping, and return later for a second try. My advice usually worked, but sometimes it took more than one hiatus for the child to relax and gather some courage.

This story sounds like a repeat of several earlier stories. It is included just the same because it stood out from other encounters on the 14th day before Christmas. Also, some parents might see themselves in this story, and be encouraged to rethink their approach to the Santa visit next year.

Diary of a Mall Santa

CHRISTMAS SUPPLIES, *12:10 p.m.*

Have you noticed that Chinese people often have difficulty pronouncing the letter L, particularly if English is not their native language? I don't know why. It's one of life's mysteries. Anglos have trouble rolling their R's when they speak Spanish. When I attempt a phrase of faulty high school Spanish, I sound like a Gringo. When I try to roll my R's, I make noises like a runaway freight train. It's embarrassing.

So, on this day, three smartly dressed Chinese girls, ranging from six to nine years old, arrived in the early afternoon. They were accompanied by their mothers, both Caucasian. I assumed they had been adopted, and the girls did not appear to be siblings. Several close friends have adopted girls from China. One couple purposefully adopted a special needs child, thinking other potential parents might reject her.

Two of the girls wore red velvet dresses with white fur trim, and the third wore an outfit of black velvet with matching trim. Clearly these young ladies were prepared for a keepsake photo with Santa.

The visit was fun – the best of the day. The girls were full of smiles, giggles and gift requests, and their mothers enjoyed the moment too.

Near the end of our time together, I again asked one of the girls about her Christmas list. I don't think she had volunteered any ideas yet.

She replied, "I want supplies."

That was a new one for me, so I asked, "What kind of supplies? Art supplies?"

Again she said, "Just supplies."

I did not want to say, "Good idea! You want supplies for Christmas." Somehow I felt the girl would leave disappointed, and I didn't want that.

Her mother intervened. "She wants to be SURPRISED."

"Oh! I love surprises. I'm all about surprises. 'Surprise' is my middle name," I said, feeling like a complete idiot.

This delightful episode reminded me of the closing scene from *A Christmas Story*. The Farkus' dogs had ravaged the Christmas turkey. Ralphie's dad solved the problem by taking the family to Chop

Suey Palace, a local Chinese restaurant. The staff went out of their way to add joy to the occasion, and entertained the family with a rousing chorus of, "Fr ra ra ra ra, ra ra ra ra."

༄༅

READY TO SETTLE DOWN, *1:37 p.m.*

Kelly walked right up to me. She was a 30-year-old woman with a bright smile. She was on a mission, I sensed, and Santa was part of her plan.

"Would you bring me a husband for Christmas?" she asked. "I'm ready to settle down."

I'm careful not to promise something I can't deliver, and in reality – I can't deliver anything.

"I'm not sure," I joked, "he might not fit into my sleigh."

"Then pray for me. I really want to settle down."

Yes, Kelly, there is a Santa Claus. And while your husband might not be in my sleigh this Christmas Eve, I sure hope he'll be in your future.

༄༅

Stewart Scott

SICK BOY, *2:14 p.m.*

Placing his five-year-old son on my lap, the young father turned and quickly walked away. I tried to engage the child in conversation, but he was so lethargic he barely spoke. When he did speak, I couldn't understand his words. His face was without expression – neither happy nor sad. His stoic features looked like a marble bust of George Washington, showing no reaction or emotion.

When the father returned, I asked, "Is he all right?"

"He's sick," the father said, without emotion.

This short story demonstrates why I gargle with hot salt water twice a day during the Christmas season.

ഐ൦ൽ

Diary of a Mall Santa

13 days before Christmas

GIVE ME FIVE, *3:18 p.m.*

A long line of children and parents were waiting when I retuned after my late lunch break. It was turning out to be a busy day.

Tess was first in line, and she rushed up to greet me with open arms and abounding energy. She was about seven years old. Her short brown hair bounced as she ran, and she won me over with her infectious smile.

"I'm sorry you had to wait," I said. "Have you been waiting long?"

Her wait in line hadn't fazed her. She was just happy to be sitting on my lap.

After we got acquainted, I asked her what she wanted for Christmas. While some children asked for dozens of expensive toys and games, Tess asked for two movies; that was all. She seemed to know that Christmas was more about giving than receiving.

Within a moment or two after leaving my lap, Tess ran back to me. She wanted to "give me five." I held out my hand and she raised her hand high – ready to smack mine. At the last second, I jerked my hand to the right and made her miss. The next try she smacked me hard, and laughed hysterically.

"You have to be pretty fast," I said, "to get old Santa."

𝈖

ISABEL RETURNS, *4:00 p.m.*

Isabel returned today for her third visit.

The line to see Santa snaked beyond the entrance to Santa Land, and I noticed her about halfway back. She smiled broadly and pointed downward to her beaming younger cousin. She told me she would bring her cousin for the next visit. Her father was with her too.

We didn't talk about anything new. We just got reacquainted, and she introduced me to her cousin. It was as important to Isabel to bond again with her friend Santa as it was for me to have her sitting on my lap. Looking at her bright, shining face, I knew I would miss her after the Christmas season.

It's interesting. Teachers in our public school system are warned against hugging students, yet children crave hugs from Santa – and parents don't mind. For children, Santa is like a loving, generous, non-judgmental grandfather.

When our time together was over and Isabel got up from my lap, I shook hands with her father and said, "I'll bet you know what a wonderful little girl you have there."

He agreed.

When Isabel left, I called out, "Come back and see me again. I'll be here until Christmas Eve."

AN UNEXPECTED PHILOSOPHER, *4:40 p.m.*

A lean, lanky black man in his early 50s walked briskly into Santa Land. He had a neatly trimmed goatee, gold chains around his neck, and a very large gold crucifix hanging to the middle of his chest. I glanced around for a companion, but he was all alone.

"How much for a picture with Santa?" he said, "but I ain't sittin' on your lap!"

"Seven dollars," the elf said.

"It'll cost you twenty if you sit on my lap," I added.

"I AIN'T sitting on your lap!" he said again, this time more forcefully, but with a smile on his face.

John didn't even want to sit on the armrest. He stood to one side of the chair, leaned into the picture, and turned on a bright smile for the camera. It only took one click to capture the perfect picture, but our guest wasn't ready to leave.

He explained that he was in Chicago visiting his 83-year-old mother, who was recovering from a heart attack.

After telling us about his mother and his childhood friends who still live in the community, he got philosophical with the elf and me. "You know," John said, "God gives us all one very important gift. One gift for all of us." He glanced back and forth between the two of us to see if we knew the answer. Our blank stares revealed our ignorance.

Diary of a Mall Santa

"The gift of CHOICE," he said. "We all get to choose. We can make the right choices or the wrong choices. It's up to us." He made his point so eloquently that he nodded several times to each of us, seeking our approval.

"And you know what else?" I said, not to be out done, "You can't make a choice for anyone else."

"Right on," John said, "You da man." Then he gave me a masculine fist bump to reinforce the point.

ಸಂಧ

BE CAREFUL HOW YOU SMILE, *5:11 p.m.*

Thomas arrived to see me today. He was five years old, thin, with neatly combed dark hair, and he wore bifocals with wire rims. He was a cute kid, and his ears stuck out from his head like the open doors of a vintage Buick. Not too many five-year olds wear bifocals, and I sensed other physical woes as well.

Thomas sat on my lap and we both posed for the photographer. Parents want to see happy children in these keepsake photos, so they tell their children to smile. That doesn't always work. Thomas smiled on command, but his thin smile with lips slightly curled up at the edges, showing no teeth, didn't satisfy his father.

"NO, THOMAS, DON'T SMILE LIKE THAT," his father shouted, and shook his head in disgust.

Thomas didn't know how to please his father. How does a five-year old know how to flash an award-winning smile on command?

Demands for photogenic smiles were heard every day, and children rarely responded as directed. I felt like taking the parents aside and saying, "Lighten up. Just let your son be himself." But then I would have been out of character.

൩ൟ

Diary of a Mall Santa

12 days before Christmas

SANTA'S NIGHTMARE, *4:17 a.m.*

I woke up about 4 this morning in the midst of a horrible dream. I was kicking and thrashing my arms in all directions.

Jean thought I was mad at her, so she was upset with me in return.

I tried to explain, but the reality of the nightmare was still fresh in my mind. In my dream I was Santa in full costume. Several children were taunting me, and asking me to say "Merry Christmas" in both Russian and German. Because I was unable to do so, they questioned my authenticity. They called me an imposter, and I was livid.

Next year I'll have to learn how to say "Merry Christmas" in several languages, or give up on this job while I'm ahead.

Stewart Scott

WANTED: DAD, *1:21 p.m.*

A proud grandmother brought four-year-old Lydia to see me. Lydia was dressed for the occasion in a full-length maroon dress with black trim. She was of average build with an oval face, dark brown eyes, and dark hair pulled back against her head. She was very composed for such a young child and her face reflected an inner beauty.

I asked Lydia if she got all dressed up just for a picture with Santa.

"Yes," she replied.

"Well, I got all dressed up just for a picture with you." She laughed.

During her visit, I discovered that she was taking ballet lessons and learning the martial art of Taekwondo. She demonstrated a defensive move to prove she was an eager student.

After Lydia told me a few of her Christmas wishes, her grandmother whispered that she really wants her daddy to come home for Christmas.

"I sure hope that's possible," I said, and gently held her hands.

Diary of a Mall Santa

I didn't know, nor did I ask, if her father was in the military, serving abroad, or if there was some other reason for his absence.

Children put a lot of trust in Santa. I think her grandmother did too.

૭૦ભ

CELEBRITY STATUS. *2:21 p.m.*

Being Santa brings with it a certain celebrity caché. I have to be careful to make sure my elevated status doesn't go to my head.

Today, for example, my assistants kept saying to me: "Santa, I've got your bottled water." "Would you like anything else to drink?" "Santa, do you need Kleenex?" "Santa, is your dressing room okay?" "Do you need lunch today, Santa?"

I'm thinking, next year I ought to add a stretch limo to my contract. I'd also like an air-conditioned Santa suit to keep me cool and comfortable when groups of children sit on my lap.

૭૦ભ

Stewart Scott

THE EXIT PEOPLE, *3:35 p.m.*

Most families entered Santa Land by the main entrance. That made perfect sense. Yet every now and then someone snuck in the exit door, even though it's clearly marked.

Sometimes they were simply trying to get to the front of the line. In other cases, the front entrance had been roped off, and some parents had a tough time accepting that reality – so they came in through the backdoor undetected. But for some reason, the backdoor guests usually meant trouble.

Most of the awkward tales you read about in this diary were the result of backdoor visitors. The stories about "Bass Boat Dave" and the young lady who wanted me to spank her over my knee are two examples.

☙❧

Diary of a Mall Santa

11 days before Christmas

CHANGED HIS MIND, *3:22 p.m.*

Tom and Carol brought their two children to see me today. I had invited them several days earlier, and Tom said they would definitely come to the mall. I quizzed Tom about his children to make sure I was prepared. I wanted to greet each of them by name and bring up personal information that only an omnipotent Santa would know.

Tom told me his son Tommy was nine years old and no longer believed in Santa. Bummer, I thought to myself. But he went on to say that Beth was only six and still believed.

Usually children who no longer believe in Santa don't want to get anywhere near me. To them I'm a childhood fairytale. They stand in the wings with their friends and snicker at the thought of sharing their Christmas wishes with Santa.

When the family arrived, I greeted them each by name. "Hi Tommy! Hi Beth! I'm so happy you came in to see me today. I had a feeling you would come visit me before Christmas Eve."

No sooner had I welcomed the family did I sense a childhood regression within Tommy. He was anxious to sit on my lap and regale me with Christmas wishes. Maybe it was the colorful Santa costume. Or maybe Tommy decided it was safer to hedge his bets; what harm could it do to sit on my lap and tell me what he wanted for Christmas?

༺༻

DISENCHANTMENT, *4:02 p.m.*

Everything seemed perfectly routine when the family moved to the head of the line. Mom, Grandmother, two girls, five and seven, and one three-year-old boy.

Somehow, the grandmother seemed out of place, almost as if she didn't belong with this family. Yet she was directing traffic and issuing commands like a seasoned matriarch. She was tall, thin, and slightly stooped. Her short hair was covered by a navy blue stocking cap, and her clothes were drab gray, devoid of color. Most of the other visitors were colorfully dressed for the season. Her smile was wide and full, yet she didn't look happy.

When the children approached me for a conversation and a picture, the grandmother scolded the three-year-old boy persistently. She directed me to tell the boy he was bad, very bad. She wagged her finger to emphasize the point, yet her ear-to-ear smile didn't change. She wasn't joking. It was surreal.

Once the children were gathered on my lap, I told the boy he was good. "I'm very proud of you, Terry," I said. "And I know you're going to help your mom when you get home today."

He nodded, and seemed to understand what I was saying. I wondered what he could have done to warrant the fiery rhetoric from his grandmother.

The time with the children was routine. The older ones were quick to tell me what they wanted for Christmas. Terry was quiet, but that's not unusual for a three year old.

As the children returned to their mother, the grandmother got on her soapbox again, berating the three year old unmercifully. And all the while she flashed her toothy smile for all to see, as if it was a permanent facial feature.

Then she started in on me. "Did you tell him he ain't gettin' nothing for Christmas? Well, did you?" Then she pushed the boy back toward me for his final condemnation.

"Let me take care of this," I said, loud enough to get the grandmother's attention. I wanted her to know I had heard her the first time.

"You are a very good boy, Terry," I said, holding the boy's hands and looking directly into his face. "Don't let anyone tell you that you are bad. God loves you very much, and God does not make junk – or bad boys." I glanced at the grandmother. She was making a dynamic fist pump. She thought I was giving the boy hell, and she was cheering me on. When my speech was over, I shook both of Terry's hands to emphasize the point.

Without faltering, Terry said, "God is dead."

"No, Terry, that's not right. "He is very much alive. In fact, I talk to him every day. And later today I'm going to tell Him about our conversation, and what a fine big boy you are."

Diary of a Mall Santa

The boy said nothing more.

Where does a three-year-old child hear such things? I know there are a lot of atheists in this world, and some want to pass their unbelief along to their children and grandchildren. But why would they bring their children to see Santa? The history and tradition of Santa Claus is entirely Christian, and has been for 1,700 years.

Santa hears some sad stories, and this one ranks right at the top.

The next person in line was a middle-aged woman, wearing what looked like a dark blue police uniform. Her bright smile lifted my spirits. She had overheard the grandmother rebuking Terry. I asked about her uniform. Was she in the police force?

No, she was not a policewoman, she told me. Rather, she was a guard at the Audy Home in Chicago, a juvenile detention facility for dysfunctional, often abused, and dangerous children, ages eight to 18.

"The children I see everyday have never been told they are good or loved," she told me. "So they grow up believing they are bad and without value. It's hard to reverse the pattern. Many of the children are destined to be our future prisoners." I was surprised at her bright smile. Yet I was encouraged that such a positive woman was in a place where she could influence change among so many troubled children.

Why do I include a sad story like this? Perhaps it's a reminder to all parents and grandparents. I was certainly not immune from making mistakes as a parent. Yet it's never too late to apologize, affirm your love for your children, and acknowledge their value and self worth.

REFLECTION, *5:18 p.m.*

My next visitor underscored what I have learned over the years: affirm your children's fine behavior, and they will grown up to be good, well-adjusted and productive adults.

Kathy, an attractive 30-something mother of three, demonstrated this positive philosophy when she brought her children to see me today.

The name of her oldest child, Steven, appeared on the decorative "Good Boys and Girls" sign next to my Santa chair. But the names of her daughters,

Diary of a Mall Santa

Lydia and Ashley, were missing. So Mom used her Sharpie® to add two more names to the bottom of the list.

Yes, this did partially deface the beautiful list with carefully printed names, but more importantly – it spoke volumes to her children. They left Santa Land with smiles on their faces, knowing that their mother believed in them. The mother wanted the world to know that Steven, Lydia and Ashley were ALL good children.

I predict her children will be exemplary parents some day, just like their mom. They might be graffiti artists too.

UPSET SANTA, *6:02 p.m.*

Perhaps I'm just too thin skinned, but it continues to bother me when people call me skinny and anorexic. It happened again today. It's rude. In a world of political correctness, some people are way out of line.

To fill out my costume, I have to wear a padded tummy – but it doesn't make me look fat. What am I supposed to do? Gain 100 pounds and become a fat, blubbery slob just to be Santa for six weeks?

If I called a 300-pound visitor "fat or obese," she would take me out with a right hook. She would be appalled by my vulgar affront.

So why is it acceptable to call some people skinny? Besides, the original Saint Nicholas was fit and trim. I've seen pictures.

The next time some over-sized behemoth calls me skinny, he or she is going to get lumps of high-sulfur coal on Christmas morning.

ଧେଉଃ

10 days before Christmas

REDISCOVERING CHRISTMAS, *9:45 a.m.*

The accordion steel security gate in front of my dressing room was always closed, but I could hear everything that was being said outside. A thin black

Diary of a Mall Santa

veil was hung the full length of the room, from the ceiling to the floor, making it impossible for people on the outside of the store to tell that I was inside, preparing to be Santa.

It was a slow, methodical process to transform from civilian Stew to Santa, and I took my time. I didn't want to rush the metamorphosis.

As I prepared today, I casually listened to Christmas music wafting through the mall. After several minutes, it occurred to me that all of the music consisted of secular holiday songs, such as: *Rudolph the Red-Nosed Reindeer, I'm Dreaming of a White Christmas, Frosty the Snowman,* and others. There were no traditional Christian hymns like, *Silent Night, O Little Town of Bethlehem,* or *Joy to the World.*

That doesn't seem strange; our society has secularized Christmas.

We have all heard that states of depression and even suicides peak during the holidays. Why is that? Christmas is and should be one of the most joyous times of the year. What is it about Christmas that depresses people?

Here's my opinion: secular holiday music presents false expectations. We are somehow told through the lyrics of many secular songs that we're supposed to be happy. If we're not overjoyed, there must be something wrong with us. On the other hand, the sacred music presents a story of a baby born in humble surroundings. A pregnant Mary and her husband, Joseph, traveled for days because an oppressive government required them to be in Bethlehem for the census. There was nothing majestic about their trip or the place where the baby was born. It was dirty, cold and dangerous.

Today, we associate Christmas with rampant gift giving. We've got to spend, spend, spend and give, give, give if we're going to live up to the expectations of society. Even the government expects us to do our duty to help the economy.

In reality, the only gift we read about in Luke's biblical account of the Christmas story is the gift God gives each of us – His only son, the baby Jesus. Yes,

we should sing, *Joy to the World, the Lord is come* . . .
And receive this magnificent gift.

    That sure doesn't depress me.

ಸ∽ಌ

TWIN SISTERS, *10:45 a.m.*

She was standing to the right side of the mall entrance when I arrived. She smiled and waved. The woman looked vaguely familiar. As I approached her I realized why. Sarah was one of two women I saw most Saturday nights at the homeless shelter I had helped manage a few years ago. The other woman, Natalie, was her identical twin. They were in their mid-50s, wore tattered clothing and carried their life's possessions in plastic shopping bags. Both women had dark complexions, high cheekbones and soft, dark eyes. When they smiled, their identical grins were pleasant and disarming.

    "Hi, how are you?" I asked. "Where's your sister?"

    "She's inside," Sarah said. "We're just here filling out job applications."

Stewart Scott

I was glad they were filling out applications, but I also knew the mall wasn't hiring. Besides, as much as those two women wanted and deserved jobs, neither had employable skills. I knew they were both heading for another disappointment.

"Do you work here?" Sarah asked.

"Well, sort of. I'm Santa Claus for the mall this year. I'll be here every day through Christmas Eve."

She smiled, almost laughing with one hand covering her mouth, as she visualized me in a bright red suit and beard.

"Say," I said. "Why don't you and your sister come visit me and we'll get our pictures taken together?"

"We might just do that."

The thought of Sarah and Natalie visiting me in Santa Land was intriguing. I hoped they wouldn't change their minds. When I was dressed and ready to greet visitors, I told my assistant to keep an eye out for my friends. Homeless people don't always get respect in public places, and I wanted to make sure those women were treated just like other mall customers.

As the afternoon wore on, I kept a vigilant eye on the long line of children and their parents. I was pleased when I finally spotted Sarah and Natalie, and waved a welcoming hello. They acknowledged my wave, but looked a little embarrassed to be in line with dozens of children.

Twenty minutes later the sisters were at the head of the line, looking very much out of place. I gave each of them a warm hug and asked if they would like to stand in front of the Christmas tree, one on each side of Santa. They left their bulging plastic bags in the care of one of the elves, and joined me in front of the tree.

I've known those two women for several years, but I have never seen them smile so broadly as when we put our arms around each other for the group picture. They giggled like schoolgirls, and I enjoyed the moment just as much as they did.

We often put homeless people in pre-conceived categories. Some people think the homeless are hopelessly addicted to drugs or alcohol, or they suffer from mental illnesses. I won't deny that some have those problems. But, I have learned that almost all homeless men and women suffer from a lack of self-esteem. It seems to be the common denominator. Imagine yourself having to sleep in different shelters night after night with no prospects for a meaningful job. We might not all be called to work in homeless shelters, but we can acknowledge the worth of all humanity and help all people build their self-esteem. The rewards far outweigh the effort.

ಸಂಞ

FOR PARENTS AND GRANDPARENTS, *2:15 p.m.*

If your child simply does not want to meet with Santa, please don't force the child to do so. After all, a visit with Santa is for the child.

With that in mind, here are some pragmatic do's and don'ts:

What not to do:

1. Do not force the child to do something he or she is not ready to do. It's not worth it.

2. Do not berate the child. Do not call him or her names. It is not the child's fault. Many young children are afraid of the unknown – for good reason. After all, you don't want your child to be jumping onto the lap of every fat man with a red suit and white beard.

3. Don't threaten the child. It just doesn't work, nor should it. Don't tell the child, "If you don't go see Santa, he won't bring you anything for Christmas."

4. Bribes don't work either. Don't say, "If you go see Santa, I'll give you candy." If your child responded to candy bribes, he might weigh 150 pounds by the time he's five. That's not what you want.

5. Do not, under any circumstances, just drop a screaming, terrified child onto Santa's lap, particularly if the child is wearing hard-soled shoes, and is kicking wildly.

6. Don't say, "I'm your mother and you will do as I say." It makes you look ridiculous. Remember, this whole experience is for the child.

7. Don't say, "You said you wanted to see Santa, now get over here and see him."

8. Don't stroke Santa's thigh and say, "Look, Santa's a nice man." It makes Mrs. Santa nuts and it makes Santa feel a little violated.

What to do:

1. Agree with the child. He's terrified. Just say, "It's okay. We can always come back and see Santa later."

2. Take a break. Go shopping. Let the child process the event a little longer, and then try again.

3. If your child is already exhausted, don't expect him to be agreeable when he encounters Santa. Schedule the trip in the morning, when he will be refreshed.

4. Sit on the armrest and hold the child for the picture. Don't ask Santa to restrain or hold a screaming child. It's not fair to the child or to Santa.

5. Take your time. Do not rush in and plop the child on Santa's lap. Take your child by the hand and slowly lead him to Santa. Do not push or prod him. Carry him to Santa, and let them get acquainted.

6. When a mom or dad brings their child to me and I anticipate problems, I will say, "We can try placing him on my lap. If that doesn't work, you may sit on the armrest and hold the child for the picture." As soon as the child hits my lap, the ABC song and a soothing voice will often calm him down.

ഓരു

9 days before Christmas

FATHER UNLIKE SON, *1:39 p.m.*

A smiling father with a full-length overcoat and a fedora cocked to one side of his head led his timid five-year-old son up to me this afternoon. Eddie was slender with a fresh crew cut. Before the child could utter a word, the father demanded, "Tell him whacha want! Tell him whacha want!"

"T-t-tra...," the boy started to say.

"TELL HIM WHACHA WANT! TELL HIM WHACHA WANT!" the father kept repeating.

"T-t-tra...," he tried again.

"TELL HIM WHACHA WANT! TELL HIM YOU WANT A TRAIN."

Again the boy tried to form the words, "tra..."

"TELL HIM YOU WANT A TRAIN."

The child didn't have a speech impediment. He was just a little shy, not unlike many five-year-olds.

The experience reminded me of the scene from *A Christmas Story*. Ralphie was a little timid too when he approached Santa. He couldn't seem to spit out his gift request. As much as he wanted the coveted Red Ryder Carbine-Action Range Model Air Rifle, he couldn't form the words.

The impatient Santa in the movie yelled, "Okay, get him out of here," as he shoved Ralphie down the exit chute with his boot.

It was just a movie. I don't think the department store would have kept the Santa around for long with that attitude.

※

TRICKSTER ON MY LAP, *2:09 p.m.*

"Is your beard real, Santa?" the little girl asked. She looked harmless. Molly was only six or seven. She certainly didn't look like a charlatan.

"Would you like to touch my beard? You can tell ME if it's real," I said. Notice that I did not say it was real. I just challenged the child. Santa isn't supposed to lie.

It was a gutsy ploy, yet it had worked before. The child touches the beard, and says, "Wow, it sure is real." Such was not the case with blue-eyed Molly with curly red hair.

Bear in mind that my synthetic beard is secured to the crown of my head with two sturdy elastic straps. I have to make minor adjustments during the day, but it usually stays in place.

Molly accepted my dare, and grabbed the middle of the beard firmly in her hand and pulled with all her might in a sudden downward motion. For such a pretty, innocent looking girl, she sure was strong.

She pulled the beard at least six inches below my chin, and then quickly released her grip. The massive beard sprung back, like a slingshot, in an upward direction and settled uncomfortably just above my eyes. It was a good thing I was temporarily blinded, because I did not want to see the expressions of the other children waiting in line.

The elves were on to Molly, and they quickly surrounded me. They blocked the view of the other children until they could help me regain my composure and refit the beard to my face.

I was sure I had lost complete credibility.

Molly was still on my lap, wiggling and lunging up and down like a cowgirl on her horse at full gallop. She was also laughing hysterically. The elves were trying to stifle their own laughter.

She showed no signs of leaving.

"Now Molly, that wasn't very nice," I said. "Would you like a coloring book before leaving?" I emphasized the word "leaving." My speech was a little garbled. The fake facial hair had ricocheted off my lower lip on its way up.

"Sure. Why not?" she said, as she reached for my beard again.

This time I nudged her away while I held the synthetic mass in place. Her mother came to my rescue. "Molly, did you dislodge Santa's beard again? I thought I told you not to do that."

She left without telling me what she wanted for Christmas. I was more than happy to wave goodbye.

༄༅༄

SCREAMING KENNETH, *4:18 p.m.*

I learned what inspired the "Bad Santa" movies today when Kenneth arrived with his hapless grandparents. The boy was a wiry, constantly active seven-year-old with red hair and freckles. His hair had been neatly combed earlier in the day, but by the time he had reached Santa Land his untamed hair jutted out in every direction.

Grandma was pulling Kenneth toward me when I first heard the screams. "N-O-O- O-O-O!" he screamed, digging his heels into the carpet, leaving furrows in his wake. The tears were literally spurting from his eyes. Grandma only gave up when her strength gave out. So Kenneth won round one.

But, the grandparents were not quitters. Perhaps that's where Kenneth acquired his tenacity. They were determined that the boy would be transformed into a compliant child that day. Maybe they thought I had a magic wand, and with one wave he would sit upright on my lap and smile.

A moment later I noticed a small human shape in my peripheral vision, sprinting down the sidelines of Santa Land like an Olympic athlete. Kenneth had escaped Grandma's clutches. This behavior seemed to go on for 15 minutes or more. Every time I looked up, the wayward lad was darting in another direction with the grandparents in close pursuit. The defiant screams of, "N-O-O-O! N-O-O-O!" pierced the peaceful atmosphere. Other parents and their children just watched in horror, mouths agape. I could do or say nothing without getting completely out of character. After all, Santa isn't supposed to be mean spirited.

Out of nowhere, Kenneth appeared before me, panting like a racehorse, perspiration dripping from his brow. He smiled, as if to congratulate himself on his rebellious behavior.

"Come sit on my lap, young man," I said, as I held out my left arm, coloring book in hand, and patted my right knee.

In an instant, he snatched the coloring book, spun like an Oklahoma tornado, and disappeared just as quickly as he had arrived. His grandparents hustled after him.

I was relieved that he never reached my lap.

ೞಣ

SANTA GETS EVEN, *5:39 p.m.*

The mall offered visitors to Santa Land a handsome 4 x 6 picture, mounted in a festive holiday card, for only $7. Other malls charged four times that much. Some customers chose to bring their own cameras and snapped off their own pictures.

Still, after taking dozens of pictures while other customers waited patiently in line, we thought it was time to stop and move on to the next group of children. But there was not much we could say. Customers got offended easily.

So I have learned to deal with their extravagance in my own quiet way. When Mom or Dad were still taking pictures after 10 or 15 minutes, while dozens of people waited in line, I gave them my special evil eye for the next frame. They couldn't see my expression on the tiny LCD monitor on their cameras. Just before they clicked the shutter, I opened my left eye as wide as possible, arched my eyebrow, and shut my right eye completely. It almost looked like I was casting a spell; the expression was both funny and hideous at the same time.

They wouldn't see my special expression until they got home and viewed the images on their computers, or printed out enlargements for friends and relatives.

After all, isn't Christmas supposed to be full of surprises?

ೞಚಃ

Diary of a Mall Santa

8 days before Christmas

NORTH POLE DANCER, *2:22 p.m.*
When the parents wanted their little toddler to sit up and display a toothy grin, commanding the child to do so didn't work. An assortment of tricks failed as well. But I have learned that some parents will try almost anything.

Baby Sheila was a pretty, well-dressed three-year-old girl. She sat gracefully on my lap and even looked at the camera. But she wouldn't smile. She sat there with a frozen, neutral expression.

Sheila's mother was an attractive young woman with black leotards, a form-fitting red sweater and shoulder length black hair. She looked very festive, and ready for the holidays. She tried various techniques to coax a smile out of Sheila, but nothing worked. She smiled broadly, waved and shook jingle bells, and promised French fries in exchange for a smile. Still no smile. Meanwhile, I was sitting there with Sheila on my lap, just hoping she would smile so we could move on to the next child.

Then, something amazing happened. Mom started dancing and gyrating like a pole dancer, thinking that would bring a smile to Sheila's lips. I smiled, but it was hidden behind my massive beard. She did her bump and grind routine like a pro, shimmied, turned around and shook her booty. It was a sight to behold.

Jimmy, our teenage photographer, saw what I was seeing. His smile broadened too, and he started to convulse in laughter. The camera shook; poor Jimmy couldn't maintain his composure. His knees began to buckle; tears of laughter ran down his cheeks.

Sheila's father stood in the wings. I think he had seen the provocative routine before. In a more private venue, it probably made him smile. Today he seemed unfazed by the performance.

Finally, Sheila's mom noticed Jimmy's meltdown. She seemed somewhat annoyed when she said, "What are you laughing at?"

"Oh, nothing, nothing," Jimmy said, in a shaky voice.

Jimmy ultimately got the picture, but Sheila never did smile.

There must be a lesson in this experience, but someone will have to tell me what it is.

ಸಂಡ

GIGGLING CALEB, *2:46 p.m.*

"Ha! Ha! Hahahahahaha," little Caleb was giggling uncontrollably from the moment he spotted me. His spontaneous reaction to seeing Santa caught me off guard, and I started laughing too. The four-year-old child had a wide smile with gaps between his baby teeth, laughing blue eyes, and wind-swept blonde hair that parted naturally in the middle.

As I lifted Caleb onto my lap, I glanced at his mother. "He's always happy," she said. "He giggles all the time."

Then, as if to affirm his mother's assessment, he started giggling again. "Hehehehe," this time louder and more forcefully than before. His hilarious behavior was contagious, and the elves, other parents and children started laughing too. Santa Land had turned into an uproarious comedy club, and Caleb was the star comedian.

When I put my arm around the child, and began my list of Christmas questions, the giggling accelerated to a building crescendo, "HAHAHAHA.... HEHEHEHEHEHE." At the peak of his hilarious performance, I felt a warm sensation on my right thigh, and then a contented sigh from Caleb. It was more than a warm, wet sensation. It felt like someone had spilled a cup of tepid coffee on my lap, but the aroma didn't smell anything like Starbucks. At that moment I stopped laughing. Caleb still flashed his ear-to-ear grin, but the outrageous giggling had ceased.

That night I threw my Santa suit into the dryer with several scented dry cleaning sheets. I never found out what Caleb wanted for Christmas.

Caleb was not the only child to relieve himself on my lap, yet the stories seemed newsworthy every time they happened.

༄༅

SANTA GETS HIS ORDERS, *3:18 p.m.*

The father and his oldest daughter were familiar faces at the mall. I saw them practically every day.

Diary of a Mall Santa

Several days ago, the father told me he would be bringing Abigail and Michelle in for a picture soon.

Today I saw the family making their way toward the entrance to Santa Land when the father rushed in through the exit door. He was on a mission. "Santa," he said, "Michelle is going to ask for a bike for Christmas. Got to talk her out of it. Tell her it will just get rusty sitting in the garage. Tell her anything. Offer a video game instead."

I clearly had my orders.

Michelle is only two years old, a little young for a bike. Sure enough, when the two children sat on my lap, the first words out of Michelle's mouth were, "I want a bike."

I steered her away. "How about a nice video game," I said, "summertime will be better for a bike." She seemed a little dejected, but children rarely argue with Santa.

Then it was Abigail's turn. "What would you like, sweetheart?"

"I want a swimming pool," she said.

"You mean the inflatable kind, the kind you can move around the yard?"

Yes, that's what she wanted. "Good idea," I said.

After the children left, the father rushed back in for a final briefing. I assured him that I had talked Michelle out of the bike idea, but that Abigail had asked for a swimming pool.

"SHE ASKED FOR WHAT? A SWIMMING POOL! I HOPE YOU TALKED HER OUT OF THAT."

"No," I said, "That's what she thinks she's getting. You're on the hook."

He left without thanking me.

ഌര

Diary of a Mall Santa

7 days before Christmas

LONG DAY FOR SANTA, *8:27 a.m.*
Today was a long day. I was at the mall and in my Santa suit for eleven hours, but it seemed much longer.

It began at 8:30 with photo ops with various merchants. They wanted pictures of Santa buying a cell phone, buying jewelry, running on a treadmill, and many others. I knew it would be fun, but I warned my boss that if children were anywhere near, I would have to give them my full attention.

Just as we left one store, I noticed a family with two small children, a boy and a girl, about 50 feet away. You would think the children had spotted Justin Bieber. They ran full speed to greet me and threw their arms around me and shouted "SANTA! SANTA!" I went down on my knees to accept their loving hugs.

That's why I tell people, "This is the most fun I've ever had, while getting paid at the same time." Can you imagine getting paid just for making children happy?

༄༅

HUMBLE BOY, *10:41 a.m.*

While most children asked for an abundance of presents, I had a different conversation with seven-year-old Carlos. All he asked for was a Sponge Bob toy and his very own lamp.

"Did you say 'lamp'?" I asked. That was the first and only time a child had asked me for a lamp for Christmas. I didn't want to solicit other gift ideas from him that might lead to disappointment on Christmas morning.

"Carlos," I said, "you're a very good boy and Santa is very proud of you."

He glanced up and smiled gratefully. If happiness is based on love, not material things, I think Carlos will have a very Merry Christmas.

༄༅

Diary of a Mall Santa

POUND THIS! *3:38 p.m.*

People of all ages, adults and teenage girls, all smiled and waved back when I greeted them – but teenage boy behaved differently. I should have learned that it was useless to try to draw them into my workshop. They bore expressions of utter humiliation when I waved and hollered, "Nice to see you today!"

But today one of the more surly teens barked back. "Hey Santa," he said, "I want a pound of weed for Christmas."

I felt like saying -- POUND THIS, DUDE, while lifting my forearm in a vertical position, and then pumping it up and down for effect.

But then I remembered Shakespeare's words: "Discretion is the better part of valor."

DISAPPOINTING EXPERIENCE, *5:08 p.m.*

No children were waiting in line. It was getting late in the day when a little boy, about six or seven, came sprinting into Santa Land. He darted from right to left, eluding the teenage elves who were trying to corral him.

"Whoa there," I said, "are you in the mall all by yourself?"

"No," he said, trying to catch his breath, "Mom's over there." He pointed to an open area in the mall where several shoppers were making their rounds. I didn't see anyone that looked like she could have been his mom.

As I held his hand, I said, "You have to have Mom or Dad with you when you come to see Santa. Do you know where your mom is?"

He quickly shook his head.

One of the elves called security and within minutes we heard the announcement. "There is a little lost boy in Santa Land. His name is Ricky. Will his mom please claim him?"

Diary of a Mall Santa

We waited, expecting the mom to arrive soon. After the third announcement we saw a mother walking briskly toward us in the center of the mall. She looked like a determined woman, with several bulky packages in tow. Ricky immediately ran to her, hoping to be accompanied by his mother into Santa Land.

The next thing I heard was WHACK! Whack, Whack. "Don't you ever run off like that again." And the child burst into tears. They did not return for a visit.

ஒஐ

LIFE IS GOOD, *6:48 p.m.*

A few minutes before the end of our shift, an older man arrived by himself. He wanted a picture with Santa to send to his two daughters. Both lived in Denver and he was not going to be able to be with them for Christmas this year.

He was a happy, good-natured guy – about 65 years old, very trim and fit. I learned that he had just had major back surgery, but was already on his feet again and anxious to play golf next spring.

"Life is good," he reminded us. He was a walking miracle, grateful for successful surgery and happy to be healthy and free of pain.

This cheerful man reminded me of one of my favorite quotes: "Your living is determined not so much by what life brings to you as by the attitude you bring to life." Kahlil Gibran

6 days before Christmas

LYSOL DEODORIZER, *10:20 a.m.*

*T*oday we got off to an awkward start. As soon as I stepped into my Santa domain, I began sneezing uncontrollably. In real life, I am known for my deafening sneezes, and heads turned to witness the spectacle. Sneezing with such gusto was complicated when you're wearing a huge beard made from scratchy synthetic materials. In fact, the label read: MADE BY KOREANS FROM AUTHENTIC JAPANESE MATERIALS.

At the end of the day, I occasionally sprayed the inside of my beard with Lysol – to discourage germs.

The next morning, the sharp Lysol aroma had disappeared, and the beard smelled fresh again.

༺༻

DEEP IN PRAYER, *10:47 a.m.*

It was quiet in the mall. Much too quiet for six days before Christmas. Must be a sign of economic times, I thought to myself.

The elves were chatting amongst themselves, or texting friends. I headed out the exit door, and looking to my right and left, noticed there was not a customer in sight. There was a small round table, partially hidden behind the escalator, and I saw the profile of a solitary man. His head was bowed and his closed fists pressed tightly against his forehead. He must have heard my footsteps, but he did not move. The man did not look familiar.

"You look like a man who is deep in prayer," I said, as I joined him at the table. He lifted his head and smiled. A front tooth was missing. He seemed a little embarrassed. He clearly was not expecting to be interrupted by Santa. "Is everything all right?" I asked.

"Yeah," he said. It was the politically correct answer. I'm sure he was thinking to himself – what am I doing here talking to Santa Claus? He laughed nervously.

Several small plastic shopping bags were on the table, so I asked if he had finished his Christmas shopping.

"No, not yet," he said. "Afraid I won't finish until sometime after Christmas." He went on to tell me that his car broke down. He had a job at a Target store in a nearby community, but he had to rely on public transportation and a lot of walking to get to and from work. From the way he described his car problems, I think he was looking at a sizeable bill to

get the car running again. I let him talk and
encouraged him by asking more questions.

His financial problems and life without reliable
transportation were clouding his ability to experience
the true meaning of Christmas. What a shame. The
joy of Christmas had come to hinge on enough money
to buy enough presents to make enough people happy;
at least it seemed that way.

"Santa, we've got customers," one of the elves
shouted. Our quiet conversation abruptly ended.

SIGN LANGUAGE, *11:31 a.m.*

After my day started to fall into the typical Santa
routine, a mom and dad brought their son in to see
me. He appeared to be eight or nine, a little older
than the typical visitor. He was thin, tall and had
medium-length brown hair. With the boy sitting on
my lap, I began my usual Santa banter. The boy was
not responding to anything I said. Usually, when I
asked what a child wanted for Christmas, the

floodgates opened for a lively stream of requests. Still, he said nothing.

I glanced toward the parents for some direction, and his mom responded very matter-of-factly, "He's deaf." I suppose she thought I should have known.

Time for plan B – just a photo with Santa. No conversation required.

Before next Christmas season, I need to learn some sign language. I'm sure there's a way to say "Merry Christmas" by using my hands.

ಸಌ

SWEET TEMPTATIONS, *3:07 p.m.*

When families wanted group photos with Santa, we had to be a little creative. My chair was quite wide and big enough for two people with average sized rear ends.

Today a mom brought three children in for a family picture. I placed two children on my lap and suggested that the third child sit atop the armrest. Mom could sit on the opposite armrest.

Diary of a Mall Santa

My first clue that there might be a problem was the inscription on Mom's designer jeans. In flowing, colorful script across her posterior, the embroidered words read, "Sweet Temptations." She plopped her Sweet Temptations down on the chair next to me – not on the armrest. Both of us fitted snuggly in the chair until it was time to get up. We were wedged so tightly together that neither Mom nor I could stand up. One of my elves came to the rescue. He had to use all of his strength to extract Sweet Temptations from the chair.

This was only one of the challenges Santa had to face on a daily basis.

෨෬

Stewart Scott

4 days before Christmas *

ACCUSED OF FRAUD, *10:27 a.m.*

A middle-aged mother and her older son arrived today. They came in through the exit, and that usually sent up a warning flag.

He was a big, stout boy, so I suggested he sit on the armrest of the chair, not on my lap. It was hard to determine his age; he could have been eight or 15.

As we talked, he didn't seem to care about my usual queries, such as, "What would you like for Christmas this year?"

Instead, he seemed suspicious of my Santa credentials.

"Are you the real Santa?" he asked in a skeptical tone.

My stock reply had always worked in the past, so I tried it again. "Everyone calls me Santa," I said, thinking the conversation could now take a new direction.

Diary of a Mall Santa

He leaped from the chair and turned to face me. "YOU'RE A FAKE! YOU'RE A FRAUD!" he yelled, face flushed with anger, while pointing his index finger directly in my face. He spoke with the conviction of a trial lawyer challenging a hostile witness.

At this point, I knew I was in real trouble.

The boy's mother quickly rescued me and led her son from Santa Land. She seemed embarrassed by the outburst. I hoped my cover hadn't been destroyed. In the minds of the other children, I WAS the real Santa.

When Kris Kringle's identity was challenged in *A Miracle on 34th Street,* his reply was, "Well, I hate to disagree with you, but not only IS there such a person (Santa), but I am here to prove it."

If I had followed Kris Kringle's lead, I would have dug myself into an even deeper hole.

Stewart Scott

A PICTURE IS WORTH
A THOUSAND DOLLARS, *11:39 a.m.*

A young boy, about five or six years old, approached me holding a large color photograph. Before I could lift the boy onto my lap, he held out the photo and loudly proclaimed, "I want everything in this picture for Christmas."

I took the image from the boy and studied it. The scene was last year's Christmas tree surrounded by scores of opened presents at the boy's house.

The boy repeated himself, "I want all those presents for Christmas this year."

"What happened to them?" I asked.

"I lost them," he said, matter of factly.

Amazed, I asked him, "You got all these presents last year, and you lost them? Now you want them all replaced?"

That's right," the boy said without a trace of shame.

"Good luck," I said. "May I hold onto your picture? I'll need it for my diary."

He had no idea what I was talking about.

Diary of a Mall Santa

A TIP FOR SANTA, *1:10 p.m.*

Late this afternoon, a well-dressed woman in her early 40s brought her two children to see Santa. She was tall and poised, with a fashionable hairstyle. She looked like she would have been completely at home in one of the nearby country clubs. Her children were eager to see Santa, one at a time, and then both of them together for the group photo.

I enjoyed the children. Maybe that's because they came with modest gift requests that didn't include a long list of electronic games. They were also respectful. They didn't pepper me with demands.

I asked questions about school and hobbies, and they were happy to participate in the banter. Near the end of our time together, I asked both children, "Could you do Santa a little favor on Christmas Eve when I come to visit your house?" I frequently asked this question, and usually received the same positive response.

"Sure," they both said in unison, happy to be asked the question.

"When I come to your house, will you leave me a cookie? I get so hungry when I travel around in my sleigh."

"Of course," they said, with beaming smiles.

"What's your favorite kind of cookie?" I asked, looking each child in the eye.

"Chocolate chip," said the little girl.

"Mine too," said her brother.

"That's my favorite too!"

The agreement had been forged in friendship. Cookies and milk would be waiting for me, and they offered carrots for the reindeer as well.

The mother was standing nearby for the entire conversation and she enjoyed our discourse too.

As her children put on their winter coats, the mother pressed a tightly folded five-dollar bill into my gloved left hand. "You are the best Santa ever," she said. If I'm not mistaken, I think her eyes were a little misty.

"Thank you," I said. "I really enjoy this job. It's easy to be a good Santa with children like yours."

Diary of a Mall Santa

My conscience told me to return the five dollars, but I didn't want to hurt her feelings.

୨୦୧୫

UNCONVENTIONAL VISIT, *3:19 p.m.*

The age-old protocol for visits to Santa Land is a nice conversation with Santa and memorable pictures. Today, two young men in their early twenties added an unexpected dimension.

They spotted my attractive elf from a short distance away and cruised into Santa Land like two dudes on the prowl. Elf Sandy was a twenty-year-old junior in college.

She greeted the young men professionally, like she greeted all visitors. "Are you here for a picture with Santa?" she asked, smiling pleasantly. She had no idea what was about to transpire.

"Not Santa," one of them said, "We want a picture with you." He smiled, revealing a row of perfectly straight, pearly-white teeth.

I was on my feet in an instant. Sandy seemed embarrassed by the special attention.

I believe one of them wanted to sit in my chair, with his arm around Sandy as she sat on his lap. The other young man would be happy to take the picture. If I had let this happen, the image would have been on Facebook within the hour.

Not on my watch, I thought to myself.

They settled for a group picture with the Christmas tree in the background. Sandy was on my left, and one of the disappointed dudes was on my right. I was clearly in the middle. They weren't putting their arms around MY elf. I was feeling very protective, like a loving grandfather would feel about his granddaughter.

As soon as the picture was taken, they left just as quickly as they had arrived. But without their charming smiles.

ಸಿಂಧ

SETH IS CONVERTED, *4:55 p.m.*

Seth was a cute, hefty little boy. He had a round face with a pleasant smile; dark bangs hung down over his forehead. I sensed from his weight that too many video games occupied his days, and not enough exercise to burn off calories.

At first he was reluctant to come within five feet of Santa. I lured him in with the coloring book trick and lifted him onto my lap. His mother was astounded. "That's the first time he's ever sat on Santa's lap," she said.

Seth was so comfortable with me that he kept coming back several times that day – usually with another good gift idea. His eagerness to spend time with me made my day.

3 days before Christmas

TOOTH FAIRY'S DELIGHT, *10:01 a.m.*
Two adorable little girls joined me, each balanced on opposite knees. They were sisters, five and seven years old. I started with the five year old.

Stewart Scott

"What would you like for Christmas this year?" I asked.

"I want everything I've never had before," she said, without wavering.

"Can you give me some examples?"

She started reciting a litany of expensive gifts, and I quickly lost interest and turned to the other girl.

The seven year old had a broad smile and a mouth that was chock full of crooked teeth. She had way too many teeth, and some of them overlapped like the opened mouth of a barracuda.

"What would YOU like this year?" I said, hoping for a less greedy answer.

"I can't choose 'cause I've got a lot of . . . ," her voice trailed off. She was a little hard to understand. Maybe her overabundance of teeth caused her to mumble.

"You can't chew because you've got too many teeth?" I asked innocently. I actually thought she might be asking for dental work for Christmas. I was wrong. Oh well, at least the teeth looked healthy. I didn't notice any cavities.

Diary of a Mall Santa

I certainly didn't mean to offend her. It was an honest mistake. She took my comments in stride.

ಶಿಲ್ಪಾ

LEAP OF FAITH, *12:37 p.m.*

Vicky and her mother entered through the exit door. They knew they would be out of place waiting in line with dozens of children. That's okay. There were no children waiting to see me anyway.

I noticed a sense of urgency. Maybe Vicky had to gather all of her courage to enter Santa Land, and her mother was party to her mission.

"Santa, may I visit with you?" Vicky asked. She seemed both determined and embarrassed.

"Sure," I said. "I saw you earlier, and I'm glad you came in."

Vicky seemed a little relieved. She was in her mid-40s with long dishwater blonde hair, a slender build, and a bright, natural smile.

"I want to sit on your lap," she said. She laughed nervously. I never encouraged adult women to sit on my lap, but she insisted.

Stewart Scott

There was more to her visit than a souvenir picture with Santa. I could tell she wanted to talk. Isn't that my job? To listen?

She didn't wait long before she said, "Santa, I want you to bring me a man, a GOOD man."

I imagined that she knew the difference between good and not-so-good men, so she qualified her request.

"I'll see what I can do," I said. "What else is on your mind?"

She paused before she told me she had cancer and it was in remission, and that she also had a swollen disc in her neck, and the doctors were recommending surgery. The smile disappeared. She added that the orthopedist said her chances were 50/50 that the surgery would result in some paralysis.

What a burden for Vicky, and I wasn't sure how to respond. I had never seen this woman before, but I took a leap of faith.

"Vicky, how can I pray for you?" I asked.

Diary of a Mall Santa

I caught Vicky off guard. After a pause, she said, "Oh, just that things will be okay." I could see tears beginning to well up in her eyes.

"You've got it," I said, as I hugged her tightly. "I will pray for complete healing, and wisdom for the doctors and care givers. You can count on it. You've got Santa's word."

Her smile returned, and she wiped away the tears.

If this story touches you, as it did me, why don't you pray for Vicky too? There's strength in numbers.

☼☙

MOTHERHOOD ON HOLD, *2:53 p.m.*

Often parents entrusted me with infants. The babies couldn't tell me what they wanted for Christmas, but the scene of infants on Santa's lap provided a memorable Christmas photo.

Today a very young mother deposited two infants on my lap. Twins, about six weeks old. I cradled the precious babies in each arm. They were practically newborns. The woman looked more like an older sister, not quite ready for motherhood. I had trouble visualizing her changing diapers.

In fact, I halfway expected the mother to sit on my lap too, and tell me what she wanted for Christmas. She was that young.

When the mother returned to retrieve her babies after the photo was taken, she announced, "Looks like you've never held a baby before." Her attitude was condescending. She proclaimed my inexperience as she jerked one child by the armpit and the other by the center of her blouse, both at the same time. The infants cried as they sprung from my arms like they had been launched from a catapult.

The experience saddened me. I had to be cheerful again. Another child was heading my way.

ಬಂಡ

MIRACLE BABY, SAINTLY GRANDMOTHER, *6:30 p.m.*

Late in the day, an older woman arrived with another infant. The child was in a baby seat, nestled in a

Diary of a Mall Santa

shopping cart. The woman gently placed the baby on my lap for a picture.

When I first looked at the infant, I was reminded of the movie *The Curious Case of Benjamin Button*. The tiny face looked like a very old person with wrinkles and bluish-red coloring; she also had a feeding tube in one nostril. Yes, baby Renee looked very frail.

There were no other children in line after the picture was taken, so I approached the woman -- probably the grandmother. The child looked like a newborn, but the woman said no, Renee was really three months old, she explained, but had a terminal disease and wasn't expected to live too much longer.

The woman cared for Renee with the affection of a saint. She ordered six pictures of Santa and the baby. I could only guess for whom the pictures were taken, but knew that they would be a lasting memory for the people who loved and cared for Renee.

I had witnessed a miracle. Both the woman and the baby were living examples of God's perfect grace.

ఐస

Stewart Scott

2 days before Christmas

PRICELESS, *11:46 a.m.*

Santa doesn't hear the familiar names of his generation very often. Names like Billy, Mary, Fred, Cathy and Eddie are scarce these days. I don't know why. I kind of like the tried and true names. They're easier to remember.

Here are some of the unusual names I've encountered this year: Bronco, Medallia, Maverick, Draino, Stinky Butt, Harlot, Pooh Pooh, Mommy, Turdy, and Priceless.

I guess I can understand why a mother would name her little girl "Priceless." The cute little bundle of joy pops into this world and Mom says, "Oh, isn't she just Priceless." Bingo! They've got a name. But to call the child "Pricey" seems to defeat the purpose.

I concede that some of these names might be nicknames.

Diary of a Mall Santa

LEGS TOGETHER, *1:20 p.m.*

A very young woman brought her three-year-old daughter in for a Christmas picture with Santa. I didn't notice a wedding ring. The child wore a flowing purple dress with white fur trim. An admiring grandmother sat off in the wings.

When children sat on my lap, most simply straddled one leg and posed like a cowboy mounting a horse. It was an acceptable look, but not very ladylike. The grandmother noticed the awkward pose and decided to photo-direct the production.

"TELL HER TO KEEP HER LEGS TOGETHER," the grandmother shouted.

I felt like adding – You should have told your daughter that about four years ago. I kept my mouth shut, like a good Santa.

ಸಂಘ

TAKE THIS JOB – AND LOVE IT! *4:45 p.m.*

A stocky, barrel-chested man in his mid 50s arrived near the end of my shift for his annual picture with

Santa. He said he had been coming in every year since the mall opened in the 1970s. The man had gray hair, wore a leather jacket, and an unusual hat that looked like a beret with a short bill. He reminded me of a biker, I thought, and was anxious to get the picture out of the way and head back to his Harley.

He knew the routine better than I did. He leaned into the armrest, put his left arm tightly around my shoulders and preened for the camera. All it took was one click of the camera and he was on his feet again, waiting for the photo to slowly grunt its way out of the printer.

As he gathered his packages and headed for the exit, he shouted, "They couldn't pay me enough to do what you do."

"Hey, I love this job," I replied.

When our children were young, they would wait for me to return from work so we could play catch in the backyard, read books, play games, or just enjoy being together. I loved those magical times.

Diary of a Mall Santa

Maybe that's one reason why we kept having children – so I would have kids to play with.

So being Santa filled a void for me. I could play the role of a caring father or grandfather to hundreds of children every day – more than a month of exhausting bliss.

I can't wait until next year.

ಸಾಡಿ

REMARKABLE FAMILY, *5:11 p.m.*

The long line of children waiting to see Santa was slowing down near the end of the day. The mall was quiet. We welcomed the respite, but I would rather be busy. I would rather have a child or two sitting on my lap, engaged in a lively conversation.

Events can develop quickly, and they did when I spotted a couple with their baby slowly making their way down the path through Santa Land. They looked like they were savoring every moment. They took pleasure in all the colorful displays along the way. While the couple appeared to be in their 30s, I guessed that the child was their first baby.

Stewart Scott

The dad chose to stand in the wings with his video camera while his wife and baby Randle sat with me on my chair, with Mom on the armrest. She was an attractive woman with shoulder-length brown hair and an engaging smile. Randle was eight months old – the perfect age for a first visit with Santa. They looked like a couple you would like to have as neighbors.

Several good pictures were taken, and Dad recorded the entire event on his video camera. They were in no hurry to leave. Because no one else was in line, I didn't want to rush the family along.

Even after they paid for the pictures, they lingered in Santa Land. This seemed like a seminal moment for the family; they didn't want to miss a thing. Dad was still poised with his camera, shooting Mom and Randle in Santa Land.

"How would you like a guided tour?" I asked, and they welcomed my company on the sightseeing expedition. "Over on your right," I said, "you have the skating penguins on a pond of artificial ice. Behind the penguins you'll see Rudolph on ice skates too. You can tell it's Rudolph by his bright red nose."

Diary of a Mall Santa

They treated the event as if they were receiving a personalized guided tour of Santa's estate at the North Pole. It was like the president giving you a guided tour of the White House. The camera kept humming. Dad, the cameraman, wasn't going to miss one part of the magical tour. I could just image how special the video would be to the family years from now.

Before I returned to my chair, the dad quickly slapped a twenty-dollar bill in my palm. I tried to resist, but he insisted. I think he appreciated the extra attention. I learned that they lived 45 minutes away, and I hoped I made the long trip worthwhile. Their visit capped my day too, and not just because of the generous tip.

Christmas Eve: the day before Christmas

PACIFIER SYNDROME, *11:58 a.m.*

I observed an interesting social phenomenon today. Lots of infants were addicted to pacifiers. Most parents didn't want pacifiers stuck in their childrens' mouths during the photo sessions with Santa, yet they didn't want to stick the moist pacifiers in their pockets or purses either. All this made perfect sense.

Here's my keen observation based on an informal scientific study of hundreds of young families and their children: some fathers put the child's pacifier in their own mouths, nipple end first. Then they sucked on the pacifier, sometimes vigorously. They sucked and chewed on that rubber nipple, even when they knew you were watching.

I'm not sure what this proves, but it was a great hypothesis for a doctoral thesis on unusual human behavior.

ഗ‌ര

BLESSING FOR SANTA, *2:31 p.m.*

An unusual, yet refreshing thing happened today. A spunky little girl with bright blue eyes and curly brown hair visited me, and when I asked her what she wanted for Christmas, she said, "I want YOU to have a happy Christmas, Santa." Her name was Greta, and I felt like visiting with her for hours.

Diary of a Mall Santa

"I will," I said, somewhat astonished by her goodness. "It makes me happy just to meet you today. You are a wonderful little girl."

She didn't ask for a single present, but she left with a wave and a wink. "See you on Christmas Eve," she shouted. "I love you a ton!"

༄༅༄

POLICE ESCORT, *3:11 p.m.*

This was my last day as Santa for the season. I'll miss playing this role. Unfortunately, I've observed that the closer we get to Christmas, the ruder some parents become. I don't mean to judge, but somehow I think some of our guests have forgotten why we celebrate Christmas.

For example, some adults apparently didn't think Santa should have taken a break during an eight-hour shift. I guess they thought I should have been fitted with a permanent catheter and not allowed to shed my heavy outfit, remove my pillow for a few minutes, and have lunch. Such was the case with an irate father and his daughters who were told that

Stewart Scott

Santa was taking a short break and would return in 30 minutes. This particular dad had no intention of waiting.

His way of dealing with the crisis was to drop the F-bomb ("The queen-mother of dirty words," according to Ralphie in *A Christmas Story*.) And he repeated it several times in his bellowing voice, using the expletive as a noun, a verb, and an adverb. Then, he referred to my assistants as (deleted) and (deleted). Patty, the woman who managed the Santa operation for the mall, had to escort me through the catacombs of the building to the safety of my dressing room. She feared the irate customer would come after me. After all, his children deserved face time with Santa, and he was going to bleepin' get it.

Ultimately, mall security had to escort the perp and his children out of the mall. The man clearly put the "fun" in dysfunctional.

What a wonderful story to share with his family on Christmas Eve. And his children were eyewitnesses.

༺༻

Diary of a Mall Santa

WHY DO THEY CALL IT CHRISTMAS? *8:19 p.m.*

One of the elves was closing the gate to Santa Land. After more than 30 days of greeting children and adults, the final visit was just minutes away. I glanced at the long line of children still waiting to see me. A little girl, about eight or nine, waited patiently. She appeared to be alone. She wore a plain white blouse, and had pigtails draping her shoulders. The day had been so hectic that this serene, solitary child seemed a little out of place – but in a good way.

The children thought I would be heading to the North Pole to begin my gift-giving marathon. In truth, I longed to change into street clothes, head for home, enjoy a quiet dinner with my wife, and then attend the midnight Christmas Eve service at church.

When the last child arrived, I learned that her name was Anita. She was an unassuming little girl with a peaceful presence. She felt very much at home sitting on my lap. When it was time for the picture, she hugged me and snuggled against my shoulder.

When I asked her what she was thinking about for Christmas, she ignored my question; she seemed more interested in spending tranquil time with me. She asked me how my day was going, yet I dared not tell her about the irate father who had to be hauled off by security just hours earlier. So instead I asked, "Is there anything else you would like to talk to Santa about?"

She paused, and thought, "Why do they call it Christmas anyway?" she asked.

"That's a good question, Anita," I said. "I'm glad you asked. Let me start by asking YOU a question. If you could have the perfect gift for Christmas, what would it be? What is your heart's desire? Think big."

Her eyes glanced away from me as she thought. "Maybe my very own bedroom with a brand new computer," she said, "or a complete Wii system with all the games. And an iPhone too," she quickly added, "the newest model." Her eyes brightened as they returned to mine, and she smiled.

"Those are good ideas," I said, "yet God has something much better in mind."

She looked up at me with inquisitive eyes.

"Many years ago," I said, "on the very first Christmas, God gave us a gift. It wasn't the kind of gift we might find under a Christmas tree, like an electronic game, a new toy, or even an iPhone. But it was a gift that we will have forever."

Anita nodded.

"God's perfect gift is His very own son, a tiny baby boy, and His name is Jesus. We call him Jesus Christ, and Christ means the Son on God. That's where the word Christmas comes from, and mass means celebration."

Anita put her head against my shoulder. It was getting late, yet we both cherished our time together.

"Jesus teaches us about love. His love is so great that He forgives us when we make mistakes, builds us up when we feel sad, and helps us through difficult times. So, God's gift of His son is for you, me and everyone – and He will never disappoint us."

"On Christmas we celebrate the birth of Jesus, and we receive this wonderful gift into our hearts. How does that sound? Can you imagine a more important gift than that?"

Anita smiled again and nodded as she nestled in my arms. "But can I still get my own bedroom and a new computer?" she asked.

ಸಾಧ

Stewart Scott

*C*ome see me next year. If you know me you will find me. And remember, my Santa time isn't limited to children, as long as you still believe.

ೞറ

* The asterisks represent breaks or days that the spare Santa provided me with an occasional day off.

EPILOGUE

*W*hen I was a child, I believed as a child. Santa was very real. Late at night on Christmas Eve, I imagined the sound of sleigh bells high above the roof. I was sure Santa was about to arrive. Before the sun came up, I was out of bed and slowly finding my way down the dark stairway for a glimpse of our festive Christmas tree and all the colorful presents beneath it. My heart raced with anticipation.

My parents rarely called me back to bed. Instead, my father joined me in the living room in his bathrobe and slippers. "What do you know, son, it looks like Santa paid us a visit last night." I believed as a child. I never thought to question how an adult man, fat or fit, could make his way down our chimney, or how a sleigh could possibly fly through the air – being pulled by magical reindeer.

Somewhere in time when I was about 10 or 12 years old, a friend took me aside and told me the truth. "There is no Santa," he said. "Your parents put the presents under the tree."

I began to see life through a glass darkly, no longer as a child.

As strange as it sounds, when I put on the costume and adjust the massive beard, I try to take on the persona of the ancient Saint Nicholas – the man you read about in my First Intermezzo. Every day, I would spend time in prayer before leaving my dressing room. I asked God to send me children (and adults), and equip me to be a good listener and to provide the words that will encourage each visitor. If the children and some adults believe that I am Santa, I do not want them to leave disappointed.

But here's the strange thing: Isabel asked for nothing for herself, but she did ask for a home for her parents and a job for her father. Today, they have a home and her dad is employed.

In the story titled LEAP OF FAITH, Vicky confided that she had cancer. She also told me about impending surgery to correct a swollen disc in her neck. She was clearly worried. The doctors told her

Diary of a Mall Santa

there was a chance of partial paralysis after the risky procedure. I took a leap of faith, and asked how I could pray for her. Vicky's cancer is in complete remission now and her neck is as good as new, thanks to successful surgery. Months later, when Vicky told me the good news, she added, "Praise God."

And what about "Bass Boat Dave," the retired Navy boatswain's mate who pressed me for that coveted craft. I saw his picture in the paper not long ago. He had won the lottery. I'll bet I know what his first purchase was.

"Yes, Virginia. There is a Santa Claus." *(New York Sun, September 21, 1897, Francis Pharcellus Church)*

Stewart Scott, a.k.a., Santa Claus

www.ingramcontent.com/pod-product-compliance
Lightning Source LLC
LaVergne TN
LVHW050624090426
835512LV00007B/657